the secret of... *HOLING PUTTS!*

the secret of ...
HOLING PUTTS!

by **HORTON SMITH** and **DAWSON TAYLOR**

With Forewords by Walter Hagen and Robert T. Jones, Jr.

Photographs by Ray Glonka

BURFORD BOOKS

Copyright © 1961 by Dawson Taylor
All Rights Reserved. No part of this book may be reproduced in any manner without the express written consent of the publisher, except in cases of brief excerpts in critical reviews and articles. All inquiries should be addressed to: Burford Books, Inc., PO Box 388, Short Hills, NJ 07078.

Printed in the United States of America

10 9 8 7 6 5 4 3 2 1

Library of Congress Cataloging-in-Publication Data
Smith, Horton.
    The secret of holing putts! / by Horton Smith and Dawson Taylor.
       p.   cm.
    Originally published: New York : Barnes, 1961.
    Includes bibliographical references.
    ISBN 1-58080-076-9 (pbk.)
    1. Putting (Golf).   I. Taylor, Dawson.   II. Title.
GV979.P8 S63   2000
796.352'35—dc21   99-088077

To Ellen Denise,
    Mary Christine,
        Timothy Dawson,
and their most patient mother, Mary Ellen

Author's Note

UNDER THE "Rules of Amateur Status" of the United States Golf Association, an amateur forfeits his amateur status by receiving compensation for giving instruction on the golf course, in writing, or in photographs. Although my chances of ever winning the United States Amateur Golf Championship are completely nonexistent, I would still prefer to remain a true "amateur" golfer in the eyes of the U.S.G.A. and in the eyes of my golfing friends. So I should like to state for the record that while I appear as coauthor of this book, while the writing approach and much of the actual text is mine, the techniques, with respect both to instruction and actual play, and the ideas originate from the professional experience of Horton Smith. Furthermore, it should be understood that the first-person narrator in the text is Horton Smith.

I should also like to take this opportunity to say that it has been a great pleasure and privilege to work with Horton Smith on this book, and I hope that in some small way I have helped to bring to completion another notable achievement in his long and successful career.

I would also like to thank Robert T. Jones, Jr., for his kindness in writing the foreword to this book and his assistance in obtaining permission from his publishers for quotations from his books; Walter Hagen, Sr., for his kindness in writing the foreword to this book, for granting permission to quote from the *Walter Hagen Story*, and for his most enjoyable interview with the author; Charles (Chick) Evans, Jr., for his friendship and encouragement, and for permission to quote from *Chick Evans' Golf Book;* Marian Benton, for her kindly custodianship of the scrapbooks of Horton Smith; Francis Ouimet, for permission to quote from *Success at Golf;*

Joseph C. Dey, Jr., Executive Director of the United States Golf Association, for access to the library at Golf House, New York; P. J. Boatwright, Jr., of the United States Golf Association, for his counsel and advice; W. B. "Babe" Crawford of the Detroit Golf Club and Western Golf Association, for his friendship and for his inestimable help in assembling materials for this book; the Board of Directors of the Detroit Golf Club, for permission to take photographs for this

The Secret of Holing Putts

book on their magnificent golf links; and to Colonel R. Otto Probst, of South Bend, Indiana, in appreciation of his friendship and for allowing access to *The Golf Library* materials, manuscripts, and books.

DAWSON TAYLOR

Contents

Author's Note	9
Foreword by Walter Hagen	13
Foreword by Robert T. Jones, Jr.	15
Introduction	19
The Elements of Putting	22
The Fundamentals of a Good Putting Stroke	23
Equipment	65
The Etiquette of Putting	68
The Strategy of Putting	71
Scoring Your Putts	76
The Survey	78
Imagination	82
The Routine of Putting	84
"Borrow" and "Break"	88
Tolerance for Error	89
Measuring the Distance	94
"Spot" Putting	99
A Discussion of "Grain"	100
Psychology of Putting	104
Technical Problems and Their Solutions	109
Specialty Shots with the Putter	117
The Short-Putt "Jab" Technique	125
Practice	126
Putting Faults and Their Remedies	139
Confidence	150
Horton Smith's Record	152
Acknowledgments	154
Bibliography	155

Foreword

It is indeed a pleasure to be asked to pen a few words about my old friend and traveling companion, Horton Smith.

I can remember, in the late twenties, Johnny Farrell and I were touring the West when we were challenged to stop for a match at the Oak Hill Golf Club in Joplin, Missouri. At that time, Joplin had two hot youngsters eagerly waiting to take a crack at the supposedly "big boys" of the day. Farrell had just won the United States Open Championship, beating Jones in the playoff, and I had had the good fortune to bring back the British Open trophy again.

The names of these two brash youngsters turned out to be Horton Smith and Ed Dudley. Needless to say, the youngsters easily took care of the old-timers. If there is any one thing that stayed in my mind about that match, it was the effortless, fine, clean stroking of the ball on the green by the "kid," Horton Smith.

In all the subsequent years that Horton and I spent together, I was forever impressed by the miraculous touch of this great putter. It never appeared to desert him, for somewhere within that marvelous motion of wrist, fingers and arms, he had found the secret to a fluidity that never knew the meaning of the word "yips."

If anyone can tell us the secret, it is Horton. As far as I am concerned, I would have appreciated it if he had told *a little more a lot earlier.*

WALTER HAGEN

Foreword

"I bore with a gimlet, not with an augur."

Many times I have heard this expression from Horton Smith, his manner impishly self-deprecatory, yet only half apologetic for spelling out in detail his careful analysis of a subject. The concept of boring, of course, was not appropriate, but the contrast of the small tool with the larger was decidedly so, for Horton, I think, never made a voluntary move on or off the golf course without thinking out quite thoroughly his reasons for making such a move.

Horton first emerged into golfing prominence as a player at the end of the Roaring Twenties. Although he never succeeded in winning the Open Championship, he came very close at times, and did win almost everything else in sight. It is one of our real delights at the Augusta National that Horton was the first winner of the Masters Tournament, and is still the player with the longest unbroken record of participation in this event.

As Smith progressed from player to club professional to the presidency of the Professional Golfers' Association, he continued to follow his habit of thoughtful preparation for every job and conscientious execution of it. Nothing he did ever got less from him than his very best.

Horton has been a fine golfer with every club. I am sure he knows the game as well as it is possible to know it. Yet it is probably as one of the finest putters of all time that he has become most distinguished. I can truly say that I have played a lot of golf with Smith and have never once seen him putt badly.

There is no one better qualified than Horton to write on the art of the play on and around the greens. He has been one of the Masters, and he has not been so by accident. He has lived a golfer's life, studiously and with dedication. A treatise on putting could come from no higher authority.

ROBERT T. JONES, JR.

the secret of... *HOLING PUTTS!*

Introduction

"PUTTERS ARE BORN, not made" is an expression we have all heard for years and I believe that many of us take for granted that it is true. I disagree with this old adage. In explaining why I do, I should like to introduce you to my "philosophy of putting" before we proceed to the more detailed explanation of "the secret of holing putts."

First, I believe that when it comes to putting, the various personal qualities which we call "imagination," "touch" or "feel," "judgment," and "nerve control" are capable of being developed to a high degree of perfection by the average golfer, provided that he is given sensible methods of practice and a clear understanding of what he is attempting to accomplish. I believe that very few golfers clearly understand that the putting stroke is an entirely different stroke from that employed in all the rest of the golf game. It is a "specialized" stroke, in my opinion, in that while in the regular drive or iron shot the face of the golf club immediately tends to "open" or turn clockwise, in putting, the blade is consciously kept in what I call "square-blade position" throughout the stroke.

How did this "specialized" stroke come into being? We will have to review a short bit of the history of golf in order to understand this better. Walter J. Travis was probably one of the first good putters whose style seriously affected the game of golf. Playing in the late 1890's and early 1900's, Travis is said to have won more tournaments as a result of his putting ability than through the excellence of his general play. As early as 1902, in his book *Practical Golf,* Travis said "consistently good putting is perhaps the most difficult part of the game. Putting calls for the highest degree of skill and the nicest kind of judgment both as regards accuracy and strength. One of the prime requisites to good putting is an abounding confidence in one's ability to lay the ball dead when several yards away, or positively run it down when within reasonable holing-out distance." And Travis proceeds a little later on to lay down many of the principles which were the basis for his excellent putting—many of the very same principles that I will be setting forth for you in this book. He goes on to say: "It is imperative that you should act upon some well-defined principles . . . if the club presents a perfect right angle in reference to the line of play during the period of contact with the ball, and no irregularities of surface or obstructions interfere, the ball will almost certainly run straight, and, assuming that the right amount of strength has been employed, it will stand a much better chance of finding the hole than if the player simply trusted to luck and with each new putt changed his method according to the whim of the moment." Travis went on to say that a grip with "both thumbs laid down the shaft" seemed to allow "the fingers to feel the club better and to be able more accurately to determine the proper degree of strength to be applied to the stroke."

Without much further discussion, I should like to make the point that although the presentation of the secret of holing putts in this book may bring to your attention several new ideas, or perhaps a unique method of visual presentation, the good principles of the putting stroke have been known and acted upon for many years by the better golfers, in particular the professional golfers of the twenties, as well as those of the current "tournament trail."

Aside from the early influence of Walter J. Travis, Walter Hagen, I think, made the greatest pioneering impact on putting. He was an outstanding golfing figure, an outstanding personality, and an outstanding winner through the years. He was both a great player and a great putter; an ideal combination. He had a wonderful philosophy, the positive attitude of expecting every putt to drop, good concentration, and best of all, a fine method which featured the "square blade." We will discuss the "square blade" later on in this book.

Prior to Hagen, many good players took putting rather casually, almost belittling it as a necessary and evil part of the game. Thus, the methods of putting were also casual, almost indifferent. There were few "strokers." There were "cut" putters and "chop'" putters but not many "square-blade" putters.

Where the expression "hooding the putter" first originated, I do not know, but Bobby Locke, a wonderful putter in his own right, writing in 1953 in his book *Bobby Locke on Golf* said, "Throughout the swing, the putter blade stays square to the hole. I want to emphasize that the blade *does* stay square to the hole. There are people who say it is impossible to take a club back 'inside' without opening the face. With a putter it is not impossible, and this is how I putt. I learned the method largely from Walter Hagen in 1937. The term he used for taking the club back and still keeping it square was that

Introduction

you 'hooded the face.' He proved to me that this backswing applies true topspin to the ball and, in fact, is the only type of backswing with the putter that will apply true topspin. Hagen in his heyday was probably the world's greatest putter and I was happy to learn from him." And, of course, Bobby Locke learned well.

Now, as far as my own history and life in golf goes, it might be interesting to tell you that a good deal of my own ability to putt well arose from my early experience on sand greens in Missouri. The courses I played did not have the grass greens so common today but used hard-packed sand instead. When the player's ball reached the green he had the right to take a smooth-edged rake and smooth out the footprints on the green between his ball and the hole. And it was as a result of my observation of putting technique on these sand greens that I first discovered the necessity for the "end-over-end" roll of the ball in order to bring about a true and efficient result.

It was clear to my eyes that when I hit down on the ball, I caused the ball to push itself down into the "green," leave a little pockmark in the sand, and then run erratically toward the hole. I also noticed that when I "cut" the ball—that is, struck it so as to impart a "cut" or clockwise spin on it—even if it reached the cup it was apt to spin out and fail to sink.

So, early in my golfing career, I attempted to put together sound principles as a basis for good putting ability in practice and under pressure. And for over forty years now I have had the opportunity of playing with thousands of golfers and observing both the professionals and the good amateurs.

Since my early days in golf there has been a complete change in the attitude toward putting among golfers in general and among the top-line professionals in particular. Whereas the good putter 25 years ago was a rarity in big-time competition, the bad putter is the rarity today. They must be good putters or they don't stay on the tournament trail. Golfers like Billy Casper, Bob Rosburg, Arnold Palmer, Doug Ford, Julius Boros, Art Wall, and too many others to name here have evolved what I would call a "composite style" of putting. They all have various personal idiosyncrasies grounded on the same fundamental principles described in this book.

HORTON SMITH

The Elements of Putting

The man who can putt can play anybody.

TOM SAYERS

No matter what the distance or difficulty, there are only three requisite elements in the holing of any putt. The first two are the geometric factors of the putt itself: the line and distance from the ball to the cup. The distance may also be expressed in terms of the speed required to carry the ball to the cup from its original position. The third factor is the golfer's physical ability to repeatedly execute a stroke that will send the ball along the correct line at the speed he wishes it to travel.

For the moment, we will dismiss the influence of outside factors which affect the roll of the ball on the green—factors such as spike marks, unusual and undetectable whorls and grain in the grass—and concentrate our attention on the three requisites. All three are of equal importance, for the failure on the part of the golfer to bring about the fulfillment of any one of them will result in a missed putt.

I should like you to consider very carefully the past history of your putting, much as a doctor might examine a new patient to determine where trouble might lie. First, are you an expert at "reading the greens"? Is your eyesight good enough and your imagination vivid enough to enable you to anticipate the amount of break on sidehill putts? If so, you probably have the ability to determine the "line." Second, are you consistently "up" to the cup with your putts, or even a bit beyond? Or do you regularly fall short on long putts, or stop at the front edge of the cup on the short ones? Are you inconsistent in the length of your long putts, so that you are sometimes beyond and other times short of the cup? Are you expert at gauging distance, especially on long putts? Last of all, can you control your stroke and the placement of the ball so that time after time you are able to put the ball within an inch or two of where you aim it, and do so confidently?

I expect that your answers to this self-questionnaire will point out to you various weaknesses in your putting ability. You will realize perhaps that there is room for improvement in one or possibly all three of these requisites. In this book you will find not only a sound practical method but also, I hope, the inspiration to improve your putting game to the point where you can say to yourself confidently, "I see the line, I can feel the distance, and I can knock this putt right in the hole because I can stroke it along the line I see."

The Fundamentals of a Good Putting Stroke

Allow the left wrist and arm to move in a forward line as the ball is struck. That I regard as the most necessary movement in the whole business of putting.

ROBERT T. JONES, JR.

BEFORE GETTING INTO a detailed analysis of the fundamentals of good putting, I would like to present a summary of the key phases of putting. You can consider the following a check list.

1. A proper grip is the key to the two important principles of keeping the blade of the putter "square" and stroking the blade low and level to the turf.
2. There are two secrets to keeping the blade of the putter "square" and stroking low and level to the turf:
   a) "Hooding" with the left wrist and
   b) "Arching" both the right and left wrists.
3. Along with a proper grip and knowledge of the two secrets, "hooding" and "arching," there should be a thorough understanding of what I shall call the "box" principle and "squareness to the line."
4. The golfer should have the ability to make an effective survey of the green he is approaching. This requires good eyesight, a vivid imagination, and an ability to recall all previous experience in both actual play and practice.
5. Finally, the golfer must have a confident and positive attitude when he approaches a putt. This requires concentration, relaxation, and control of the nerves—assets that are best developed by the recollection of the physical action of previous successful putting.

These points may seem difficult to understand at first, but if you will proceed through the following pages, you will understand them exactly.

The First Secret: "Hooding"

"Hooding" is the term given to the necessary *counterclockwise* turn of the left wrist during the backswing of the putting stroke. This slight rotation is applied in order to keep the blade of the putter constantly perpendicular or "square to the line" of the putt. At the same time as this "hooding" action is applied, you should have the sensation of pushing the blade back with the left hand so as to keep it low and level to the turf.

The Fundamentals of a Good Putting Stroke

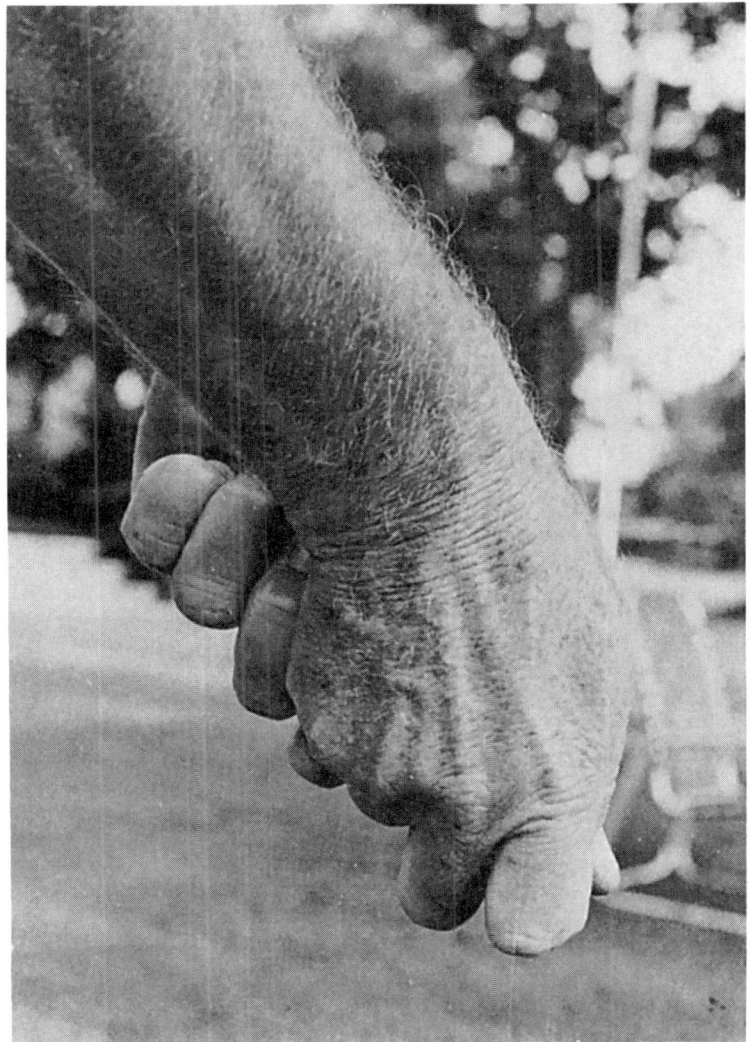

THE SECOND SECRET: "ARCHING"

Here is the second "secret" of the putting stroke: arching of the wrists downward. This is a view from behind the hands, looking toward the line of the putt. Note the definite downward curve of the right wrist. "Arching" positions your wrists so that you will tend to utilize only the "back-and-forth" hinges of the wrists.

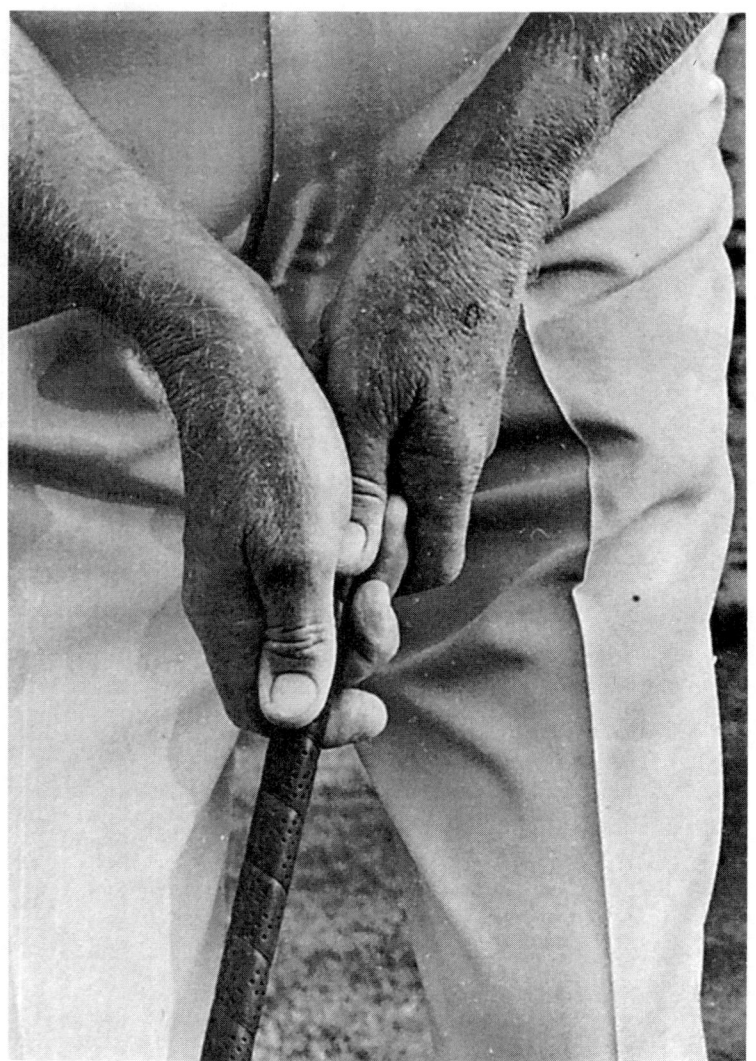

A Close-up of "Hooding"

A few more words about "hooding": in the illustration above note particularly the position of the left wrist. The photographs at the right show the blade being taken away from the ball, low and level to the turf (or to the yardstick in this example). In order to keep the blade parallel to the inch markers on the yardstick, it has been necessary for the left wrist to turn slightly counterclockwise, resulting in the "hooding" of the face of the putter blade.

The Fundamentals of a Good Putting Stroke 27

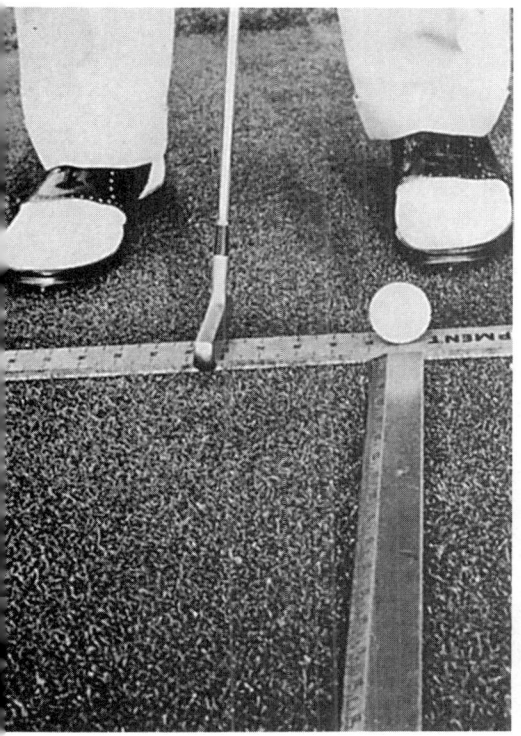

SEQUENCE VIEWS OF THE EFFECT OF "HOODING"

Here are two consecutive views of the "squareness to the line" of the blade at the starting position and at the back of the backswing. Notice that the inch markers on the yardstick are constantly parallel to the putter blade. Notice also that the position of the feet is also "square to the line."

THE "SQUARE BLADE" AND THE "RIGHT-ANGLE" PRINCIPLE

Here is a visual representation of the putter blade at a right angle to the prospective line of the putt. Note that the putter blade is parallel to the ruler that is laid at a right angle to the putting line. The blade should stay at a right angle throughout the putting stroke.

The Fundamentals of a Good Putting Stroke

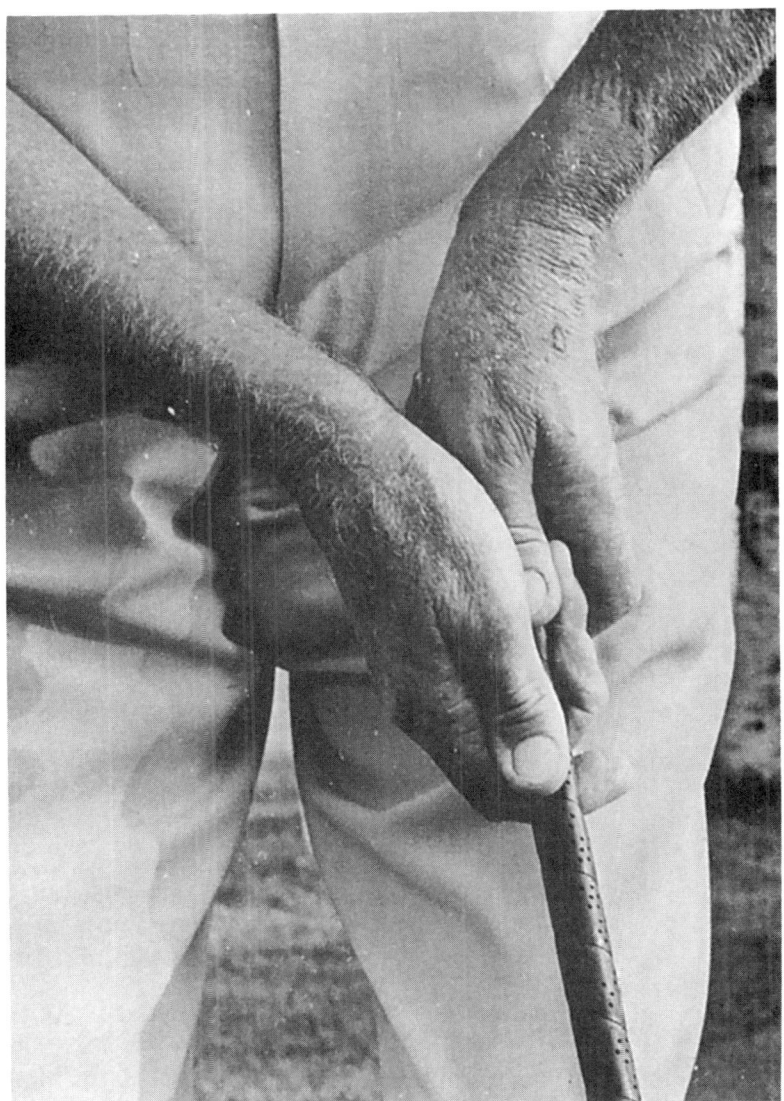

The Position of the Hands in the Follow-Through

The hands should attempt to keep the blade in a constantly "square-blade" position, even after the ball has been struck. In the follow-through the blade should be kept low and no "break" should occur in the left wrist. At the same time, the back of the left hand as well as the palm of the right hand should stay at a right angle to the line of the putt.

The "Box" Principle of the Putting Stroke

Through an understanding of the "box" principle of the putting stroke you will be able to achieve a sound mechanical foundation. The "box" principle is based upon a concept that I call "squareness to the putting line," a "squareness" which governs every aspect of the putting stance—the feet, the shoulders, the hips, and an imaginary plane of glass passing through the breadth of each hand: all these should be perpendicular to the putting line. The position of the hands is the key to the "box" principle, for the back of the left hand and the downwardly arched palm of the right hand should always face the hole, at the start of the stroke, at the moment of impact, and throughout the backswing.

The Fundamentals of a Good Putting Stroke 31

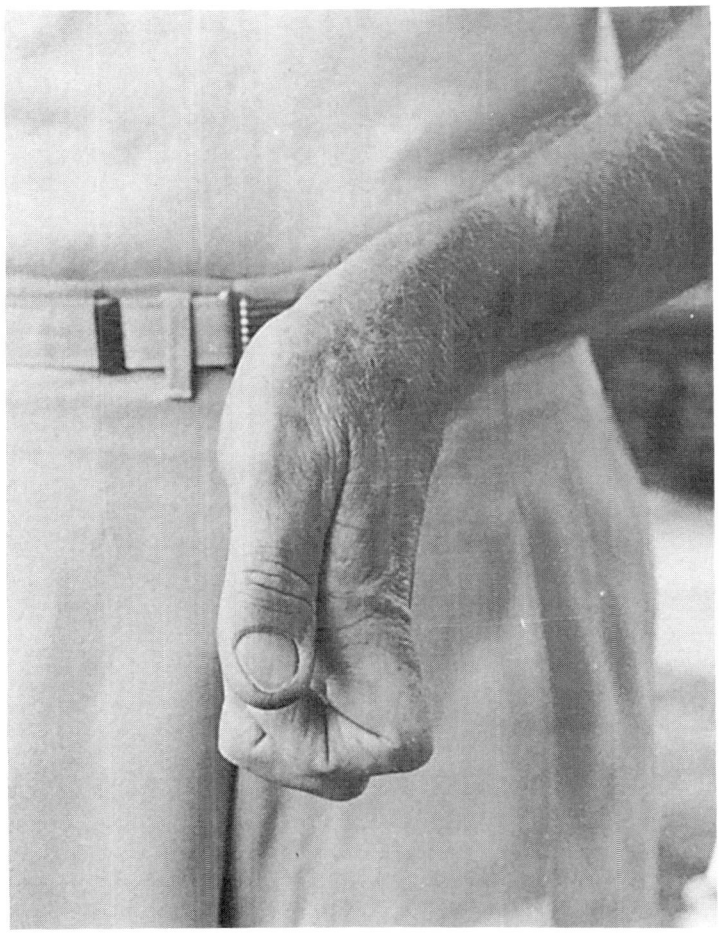

The Grip

Now that we have reviewed the concepts of "hooding," "arching," and the all-important "squareness to the line," let's cover the fundamentals of the putting stroke. You will see that these concepts I have introduced govern every aspect of sound putting.

Illustrated above is a view of the left hand alone in the proper putting grip. Note that the back of the hand is perpendicular to the intended line of the putt. You should imagine that a plane of glass has been passed through the back of the left hand and extended through the pad or third section of the forefinger of the left hand, and that this plane of glass is at a perfect right angle to the line of the putt.

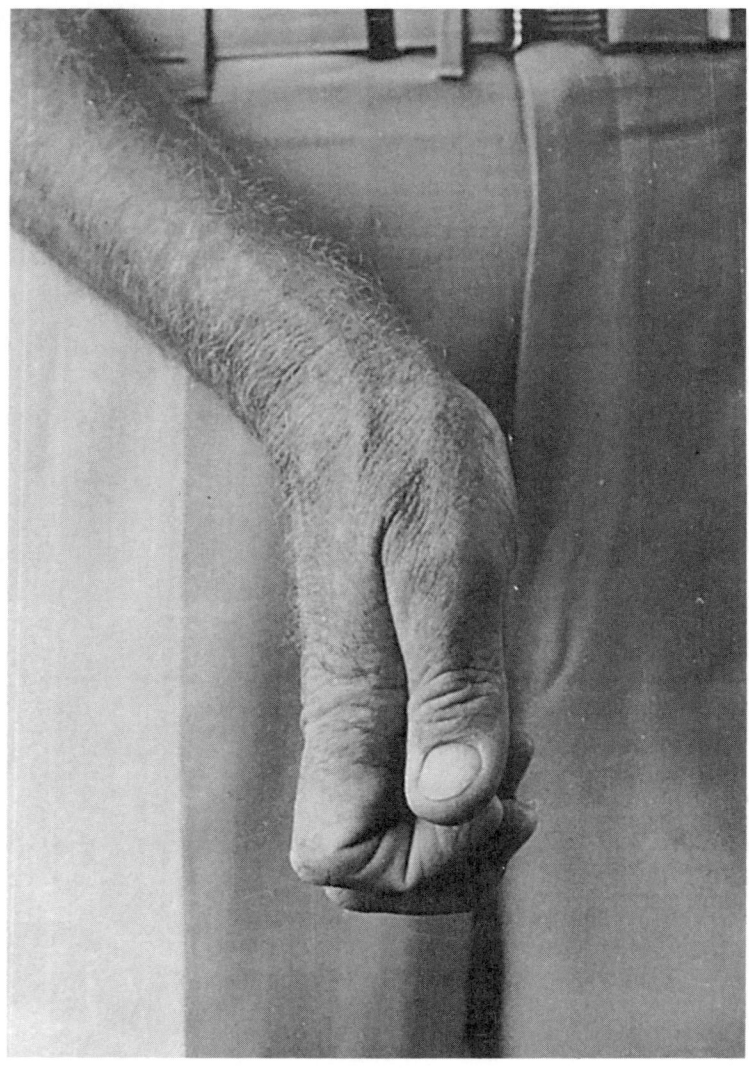

This is a view of the right hand alone. Again, note the straight line of the back of the hand and its "squareness to the intended line" of the putt. The thumb should be placed directly on top of the shaft of the club and applied very delicately. Most of the "feeling" should be located in the fingers and particularly in the "pad" of your right forefinger. Again you should imagine that a plane of glass has been passed through the pad of the forefinger and all the bones at the back of the right hand, and that this plane of glass is at a perfect right angle to the intended line of the putt.

The Fundamentals of a Good Putting Stroke

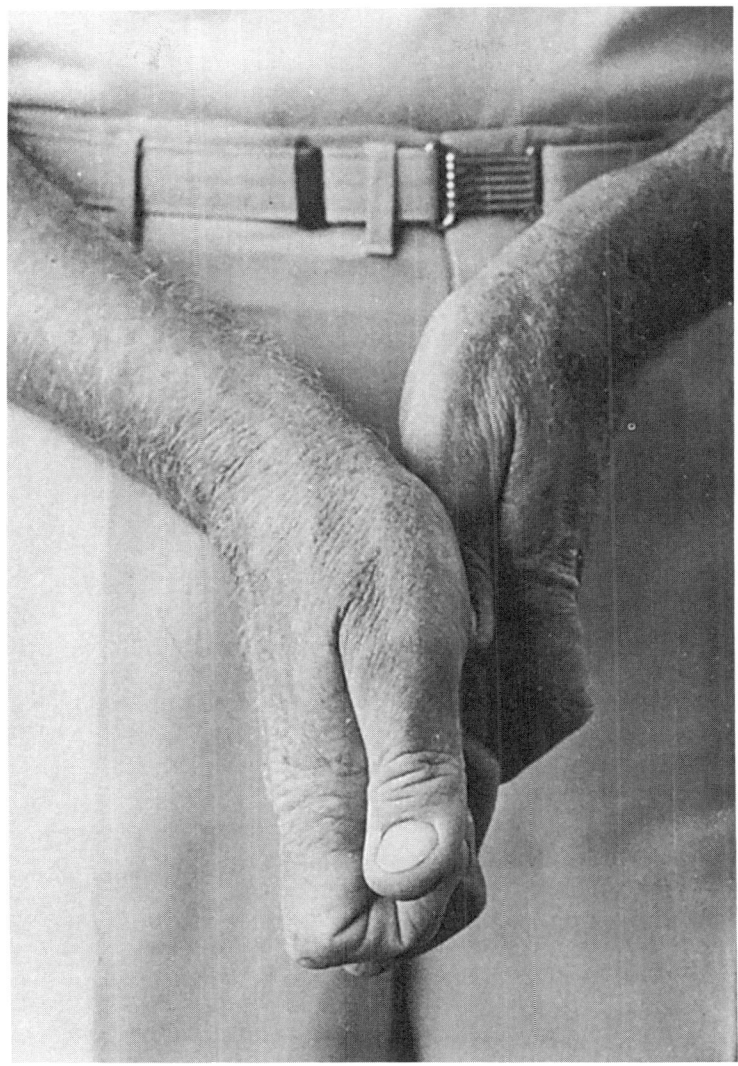

Here is a view of the proper putting grip with both hands applied to an imaginary club. Note that both thumbs would be placed directly along the "shaft." Personally, I recommend the reverse of the standard "Vardon grip," in which the little finger of the *right* hand overlaps the forefinger of the *left* hand. In this case, the forefinger of your *left* hand should lightly overlap the little finger of your *right* hand. This grip increases the amount of control of the right hand by allowing more of the right hand to come in contact with the shaft.

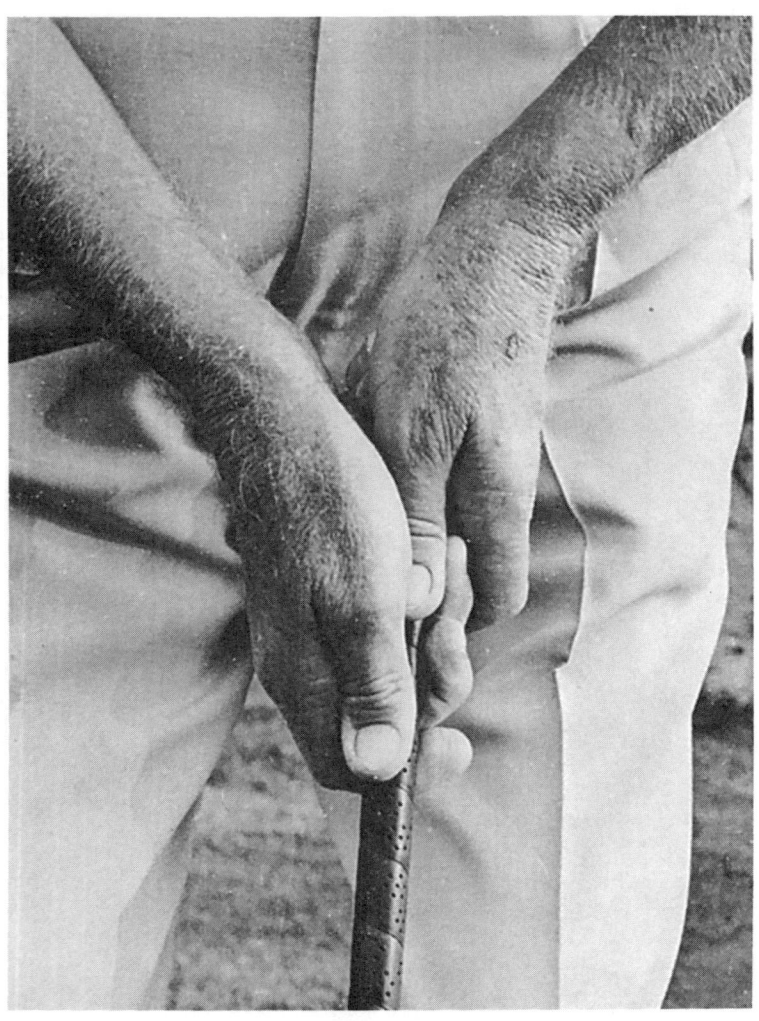

Now let's put both hands on the shaft of the putter. You should have the feeling that the butt-end of the putter is suspended from, and firmly anchored to, the heel of your left hand. The grip of the left hand is almost a "palm" grip, with the shaft of the club running diagonally across the fingers up into the heel of the hand. The grip of the left hand is quite firm in contrast with the grip of the right hand, which should hold the club almost delicately in the fingers.

The Fundamentals of a Good Putting Stroke

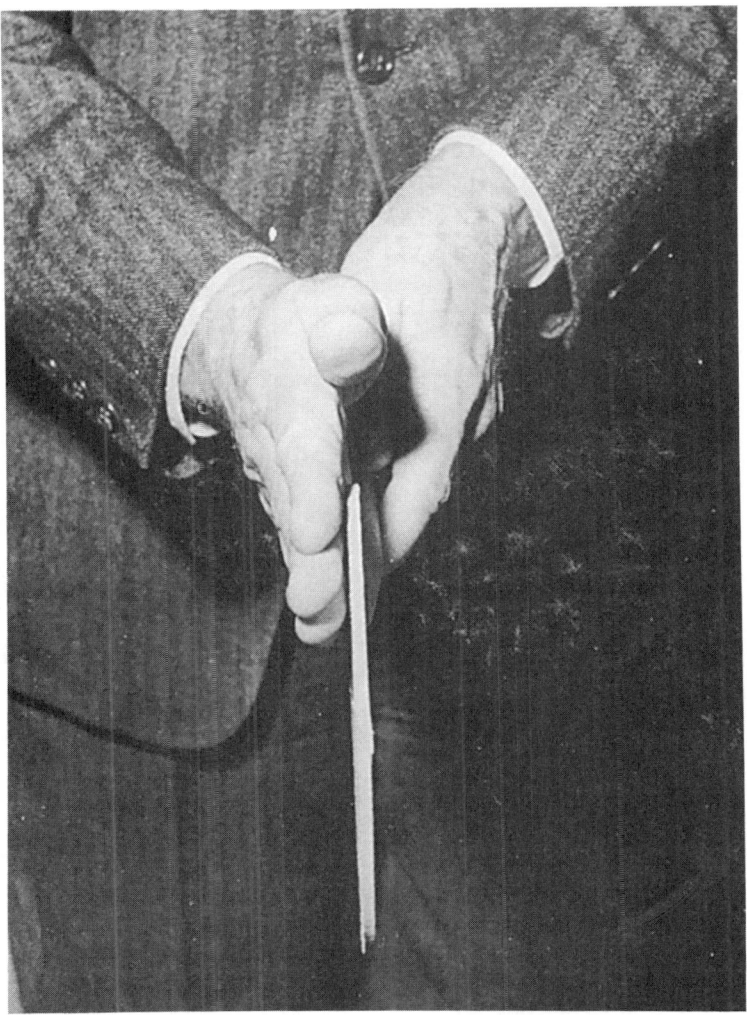

THE TWO HINGES OF THE WRISTS

The wrists are capable of bending in two directions: up and down and forward and backward. An effort should be made to reduce the "up-and-down" action of the wrists to a minimum. Only the "forward-and-backward" hinges should come into play. Incidentally, most of the hinging action should occur in the right wrist, while the left wrist should be kept as immobile as possible. In order to reduce the "up-and-down" action of the wrists to a minimum, you should employ the technique of "arching," which was described on page 25.

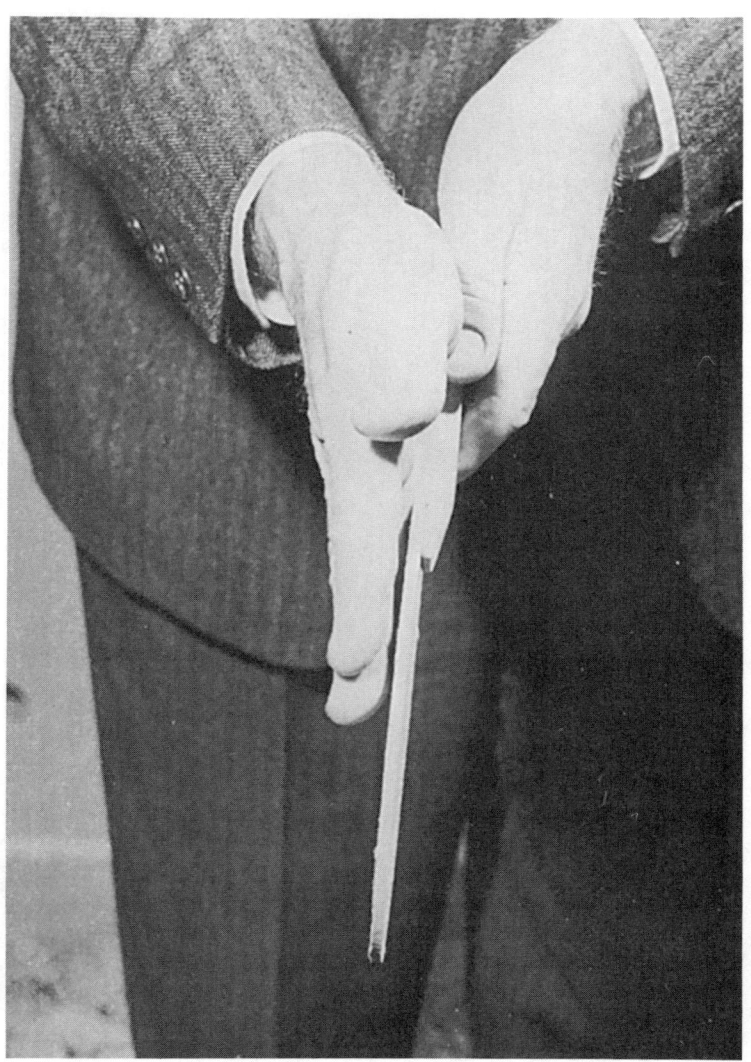

A Further Explanation of "Arching"

In this and the preceding photograph, I have taken a Ping-pong paddle and held it first away from my body and then downward, in the manner in which I would hold my putter. Take a Ping-pong paddle yourself and try holding it in these two positions. You will notice that when you hold the paddle in the second position, with the wrists arched, your wrist movement is restricted to the "back-and-forth" axis, and you are prevented from turning or rotating your hands away from the perpendicular line of the putt.

The Fundamentals of a Good Putting Stroke

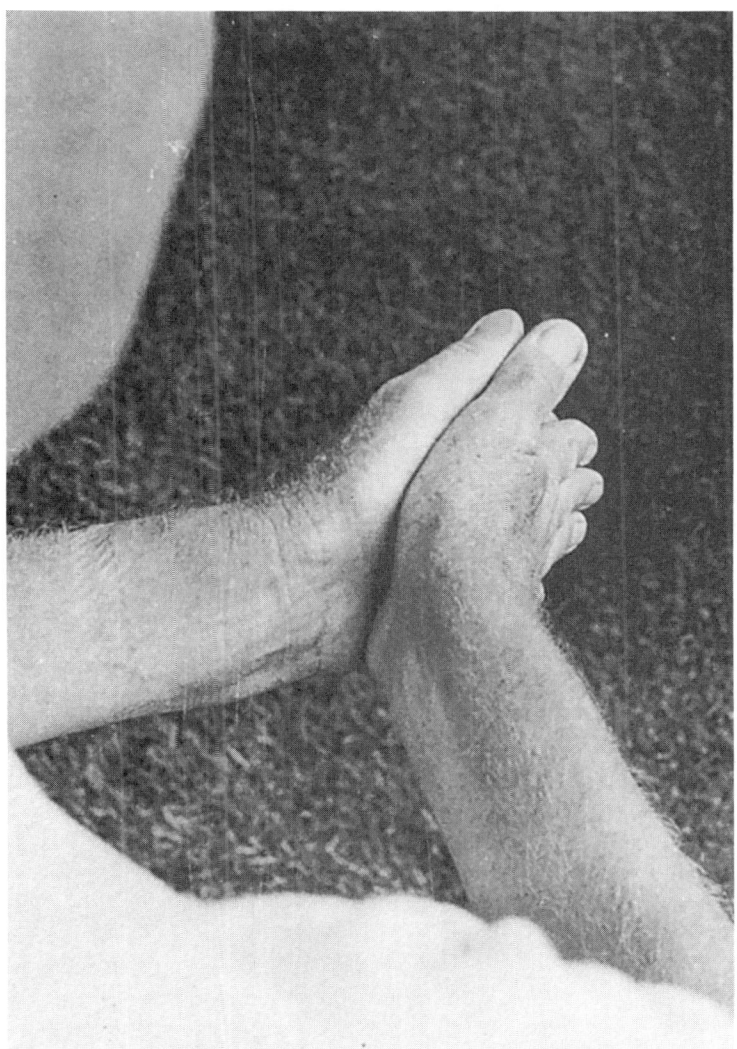

Next, try this exercise to impress upon your mind the "square-blade" principle. Place your palms together and pretend that you are pressing a plate of glass between them. There is a slight tendency for your fingers to point toward the ground, resulting in what I call the "arching of the wrists"—a very important point that I will explain as we go along.

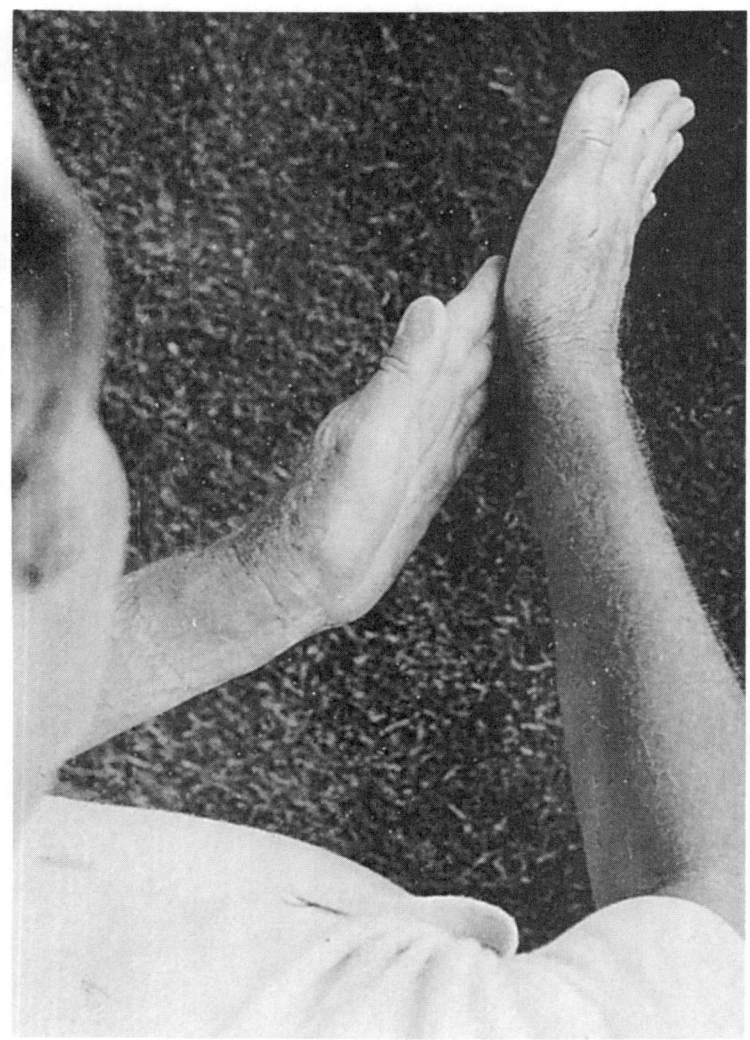

Now, still keeping pressure on each palm, slide your right hand downward until the heel of your right hand is barely touching the fingertips of your left hand. If you move your arms back and forth without breaking your wrists you will gain a mental picture of the "square-blade" principle. The important thing to realize is that a plane passing through the backs of your two hands and extended to the ground should move along the ground at right angles to the line of the putt.

The Fundamentals of a Good Putting Stroke 39

Here is another illustration of the correct position of the right hand. Notice both the downward arch of the right wrist and the fact that a plane extended from the right hand to the ground would be perpendicular to the line of the putt. During the backswing of the putt this plane would move away from this position and still be "square to the line." It should return to exactly the same position at the point of impact. You should now have the foundations of the "box" principle in your mind.

Here is a view of the right hand alone at the end of the backswing and about to start its downward stroke. Note again the continuing "squareness to the line."

This is a demonstration of the right hand a second or so after the moment of impact. It illustrates the necessary "squareness" of the follow-through. Naturally, the ball leaves the face of the club very quickly. Nevertheless, you should sustain the mental image of this continuing "squareness" long after the stroke has been made. The left hand and wrist will be offering resistance to the right hand, which is doing the stroking, and by their firmness will prevent the putter blade from twisting out of line in any way. It will help you to practice these right-hand movements that I have illustrated here and on the preceding pages.

This is an illustration of incorrect wrist action in the right hand. As I pointed out on page 35, downward "arching" of the right wrist helps to reduce movement of the wrists to the back-and-forth axis. Here, however, up-and-down movement of the wrist has been allowed, with the result that the blade of the putter is lifted from the turf and the face of the blade rotates away from its perpendicular position.

This is a view of the left hand and wrist at impact. The left wrist should be very firm and unyielding to the force of the right hand while the latter is "stroking" the ball. The left hand and wrist are carried "through the ball" in a constantly "square" position. The distance of the follow-through depends, of course, upon the length of the putt. The longer the putt, the longer the follow-through; but no matter how long the follow-through is, you should still have the sensation that your left wrist has not "broken" in any way until your stroke has long since sent the ball on its way.

Here is a view of the way the knees should look in the proper putting stance. The position is known as "sitting down" to the ball. I believe that this relaxed knee position adds to the over-all feeling of freedom during the stroke that is so very necessary for consistently good results. Note, too, the placement of the ball exactly opposite the so-called "sweet spot" of the putter blade. Notice how squarely behind the ball the putter is soled.

The Fundamentals of a Good Putting Stroke

Here is a full view of the proper putting stance. The eyes should be almost directly over the ball, and the head should be held motionless. Notice the straight line formed by the two forearms and the shaft of the putter. It is also important that an imaginary line passing through both elbows would run parallel to the line of the putt. Notice how the right arm and elbow are tucked in close to the right side of the body. The right arm is not actually touching the body. It gains its support from the upper right arm, which is close to the body.

Here is a view of the putter blade in its "square-to-the-line" position. It is placed perfectly level to the turf, with neither the heel nor the toe raised from the green. The ball is directly opposite the "sweet spot" on the putter blade. Incidentally, if you have marked your ball on the green, you might consider replacing it with the maker's name at its "equator" to remind yourself to stroke and roll the ball end over end.

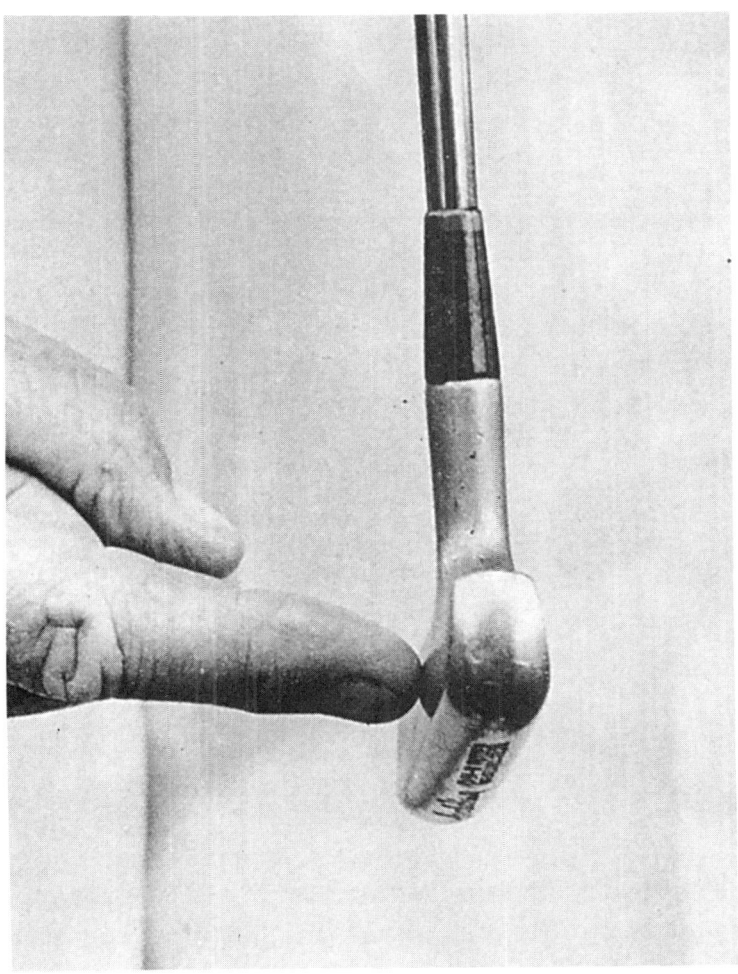

How to Find the "Sweet Spot" on Your Putter

I have mentioned the "sweet spot" of the putter several times now. Here's how to find that spot on the blade where maximum hitting power is generated. Suspend your putter from its end, holding it lightly between the thumb and forefinger of your left hand, and let it swing gently like a pendulum. With your right forefinger extended, strike the blade in various spots near its center. You will find that at only one spot does the blade refuse to turn away in either direction. This is the "sweet spot." I suggest that you mark the spot with a corresponding line on the top of your putting blade and that you always try to stroke your putts at the point where this "sweet spot" lies.

How to Locate the Proper "Spot" for Your Ball

First assume a "square stance" with your feet at right angles to the line of the prospective putt. In the "square stance" your feet are parallel to each other and at right angles to the line of the putt. You should then imagine that each foot has a line bisecting it—a line running from your heels through your toes and intersecting the putting line at an exact right angle. Now, place your putter on the line just inside your left instep and, keeping it "square" and in line with your imaginary right-angle line, advance your putter to a position directly underneath your eyes. That is the correct location for the ball.

The Fundamentals of a Good Putting Stroke   49

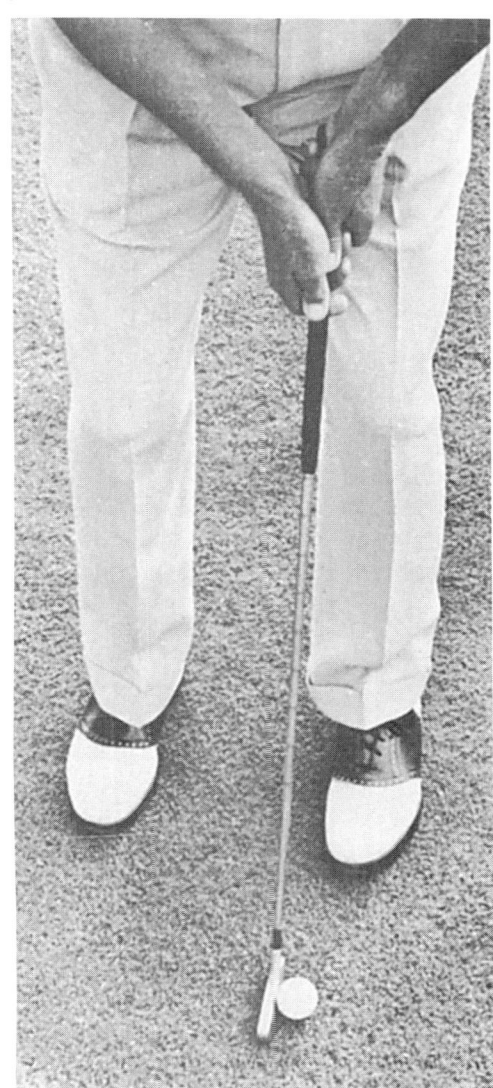

ANOTHER VIEW OF THE PROPER LOCATION FOR YOUR BALL

Here are two more pictures illustrating the way I locate the ball from off the inside of my left foot. I slide the putter forward "square to the line." Remember that your head is directly over the ball and will remain motionless throughout the stroke.

These photographs illustrate what I mean by a low, level-to-the-turf stroke. They are slightly exaggerated inasmuch as the putter blade in the actual stroke should be slightly above the level of the grass but definitely brushing the tips of the blades of grass. You will note that in each view the blade has remained "square to the line." This is accomplished by the "hooding action" of the left wrist and a definite low, backward push with the back of the left hand. There should be no sensation whatsoever of lifting with the right hand.

The Fundamentals of a Good Putting Stroke 51

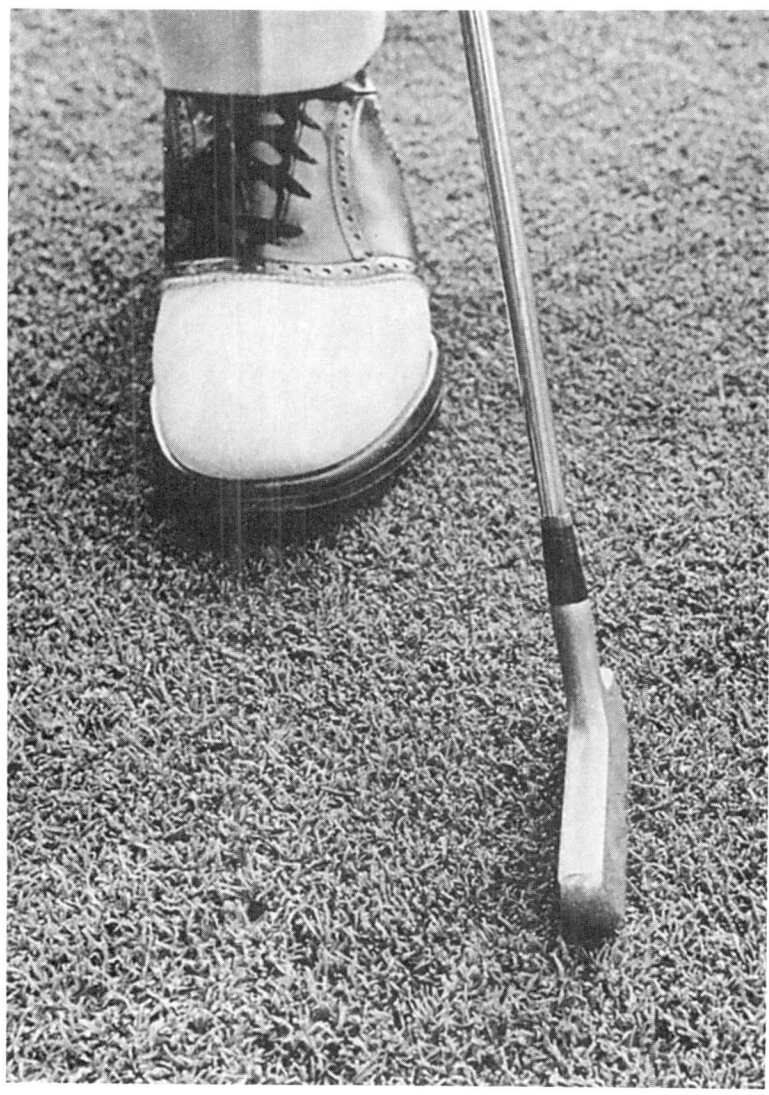

This is an exaggerated view, but the mind's eye should have this picture of the blade remaining "square" to the line long after the putt has been sent on its way. You should have the feeling that the blade is still low and level to the turf.

The Secret of Holing Putts

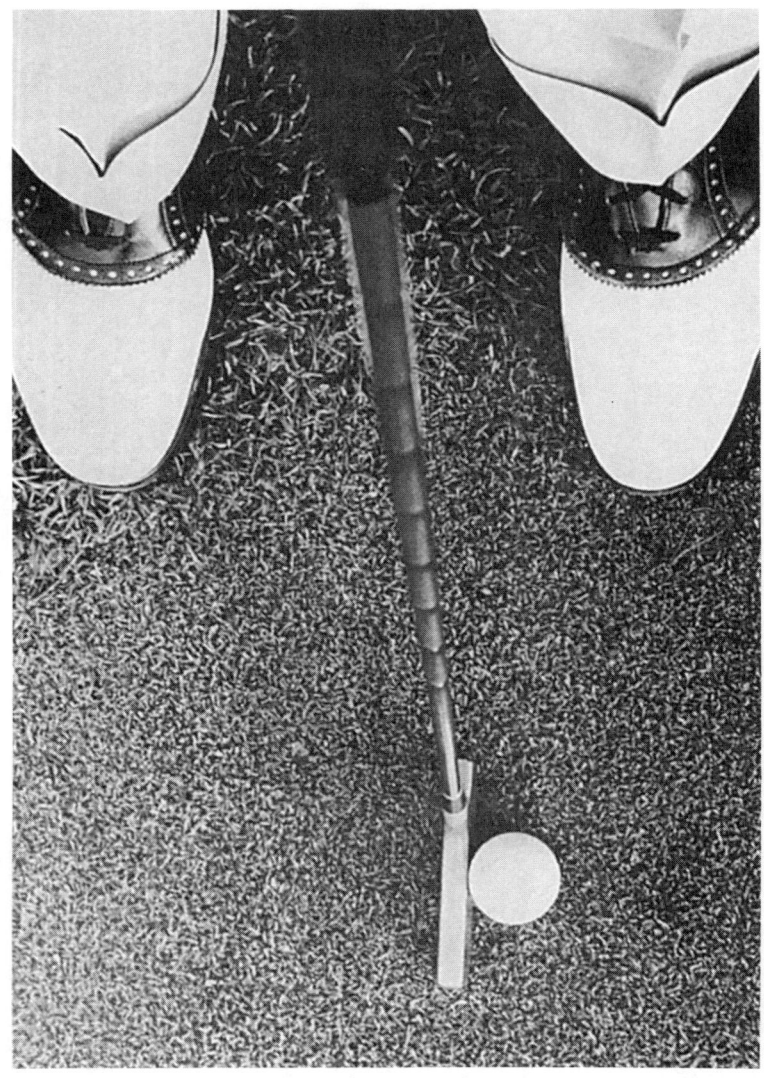

This is the golfer's-eye view of a putt. Your eyes should be fixed on the back of the ball at the precise spot on the ball's "equator" where you are going to stroke it with the "sweet spot" of your putter. Your head should remain motionless throughout the stroke and long after the ball has been sent rolling on its line.

The Fundamentals of a Good Putting Stroke 53

This series of pictures represents the correct "end-over-end" roll of the ball when it is properly struck at its equator by the "square" blade with the firm left hand and with a "square" follow-through. When the ball is sent on its way with topspin or "end-over-end" roll, it holds its intended line better and actually seems to hunt the cup. In stroking the ball, I find it helpful to think of it not as a sphere but as a wheel that is to be rolled into the hole.

When, for any number of reasons, the ball is struck off center, the resulting "wobble," which can occur in either direction, will prevent the ball from running truly, as well as cause it to "spin out" when it hits the edge of the cup.

This picture illustrates the roll of a so-called "cut" putt. The ball is spinning clockwise as a result of being hit from *outside* the true line of the putt.

This picture illustrates the opposite type of spin. It is a "hooked" putt, or one that results from the ball being hit from *inside* the intended line of the stroke.

The Fundamentals of a Good Putting Stroke

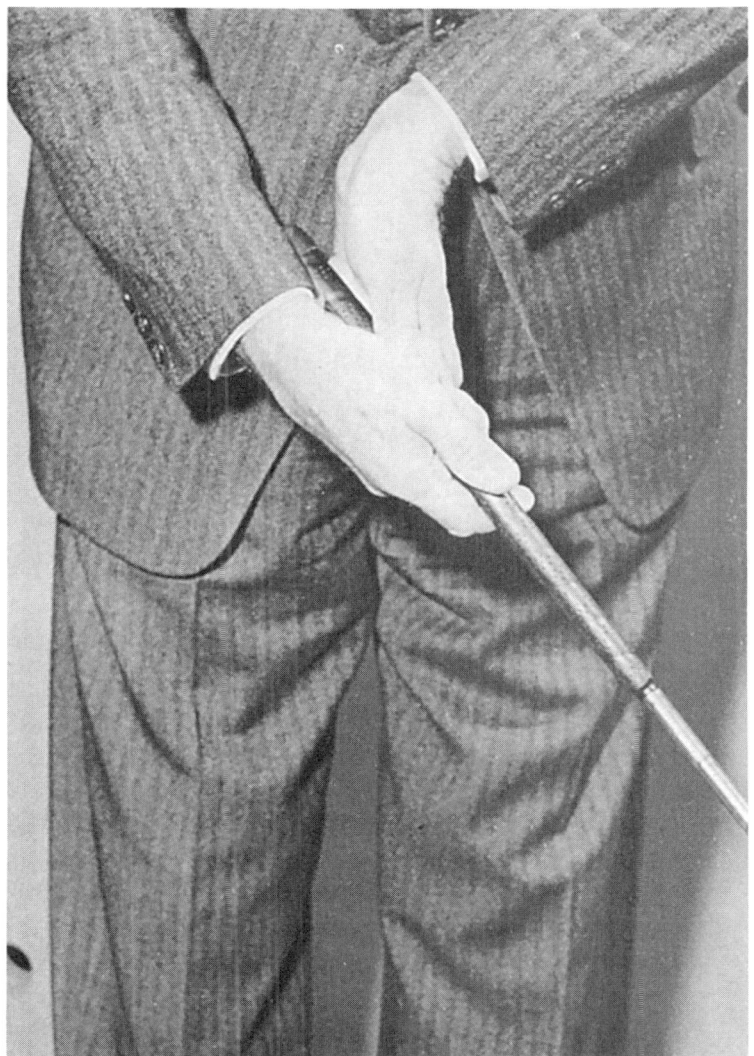

THE FIRST BASIC TYPE OF PUTTING STROKE

In all my years of experience, I have seen just three basic types of putting strokes that were effective. The first, illustrated above, is the "wristy" type of stroke, in which the arms are held fairly steady and the wrists alone move on their "hinges." This stroke can be very effective in keeping the club face on a straight line, but it leaves a great deal to be desired as far as judgment of distance is concerned.

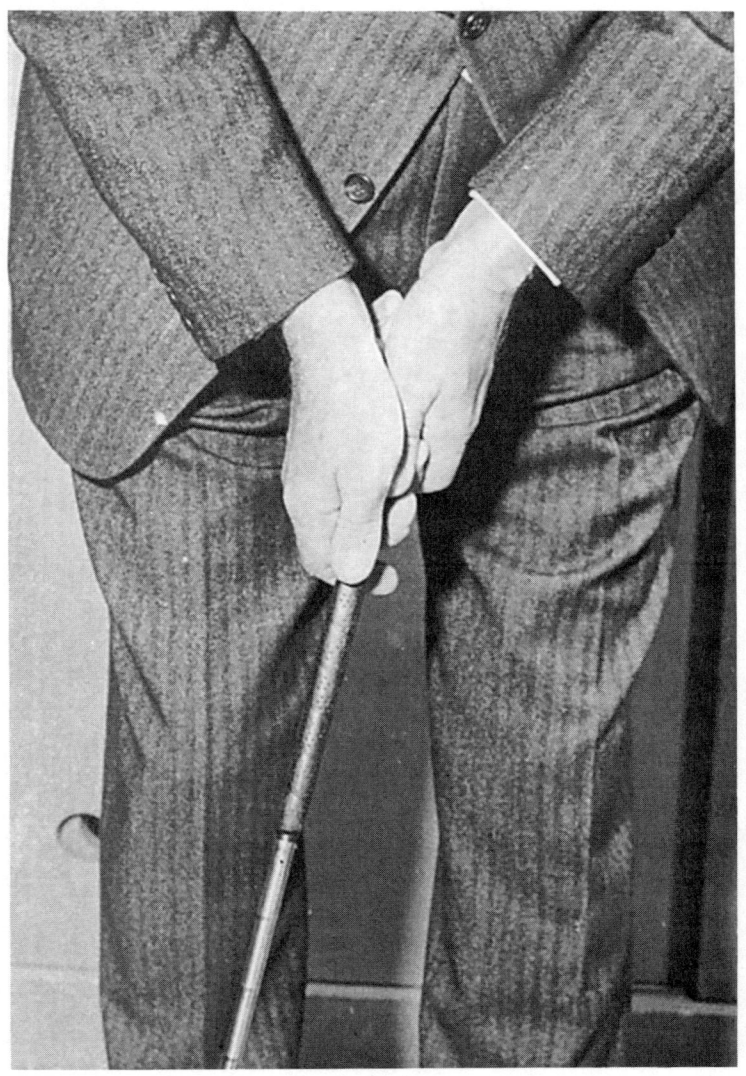

The Second Basic Type of Stroke—The Arm Stroke

The complete opposite of the wrist stroke is the "arm stroke," in which the wrists are held almost completely steady. By a pendulum action of the arms and shoulders the club is moved backward and forward in its arc. This type of stroke, in my opinion, sacrifices the delicate sense of touch and a fine discrimination of distance.

The Fundamentals of a Good Putting Stroke

My Stroke—The Combination Wrist-and-Arm Stroke

I have developed a low, level-to-the-turf stroke which keeps the putter head low on its way back and requires no adjustment for the forward stroke. Utilizing all the principles that I have introduced so far, this stroke combines the use of the arms and the wrists. It allows my full attention to be focused on "feeling." Furthermore, this low or "level-blade" method results in the most sensitive stroke, which propels the true overspinning ball that "hunts the cup."

An Exercise to Help You Get the "Touch" and "Feel" of End-Over-End Roll

I want you to practice stroking the ball with the right hand alone. Hold your putter at the end and keep your grip perfectly "square" as usual. First bring your putter back to various points along the route of the backswing. Stop it at one of these points; then allow it to swing through the ball.

An Exercise for Developing a "Sense of Alignment"

I would like you to grasp the putter with your right hand only. Place your blade in its proper position behind the ball and just touching it. Grasping the top end of your putter, *push* the ball into the hole from a distance of not more than a foot or so. Then gradually lengthen your distance to 3 or 4 feet or more. You will soon begin to understand the necessity for the low-level follow-through in order to keep the ball on its line. You will also begin to get the feel of the end-over-end rolling ball. If you can get a ball and mark it the way we have done in our example on page 53, it will be much easier, for your eye will quickly tell from the "wobble" of the ball whether or not you are stroking the ball in a truly straight line.

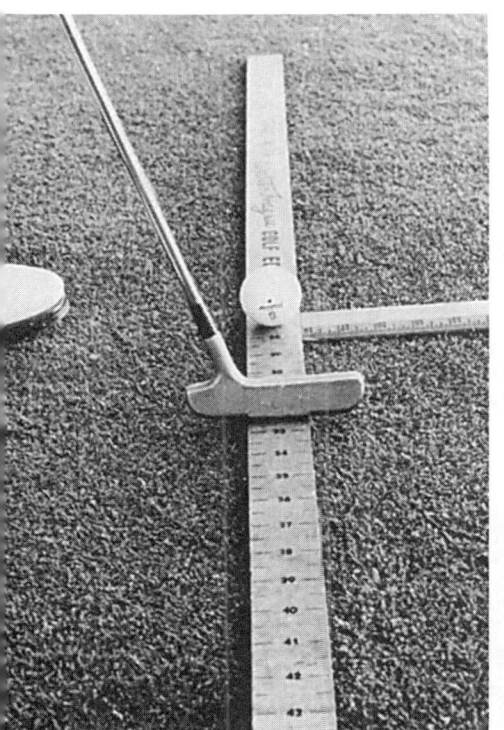 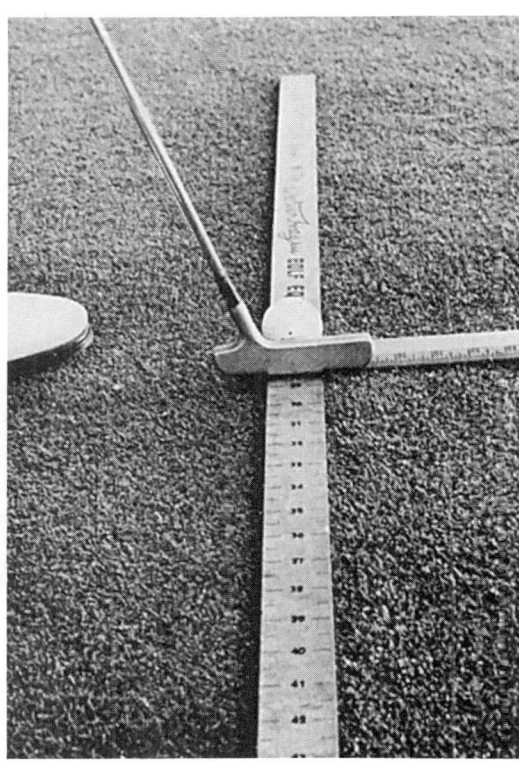

ANOTHER EXERCISE FOR DEVELOPING A BALANCED STROKE

Take a yardstick, and, in the manner illustrated above, practice moving the blade of your putter back to about 4 inches from your starting point and then forward about 4 inches beyond your starting point. At each point along your backswing, while your blade is moving both forward and backward, stop to check the position of your blade. It should at all times be parallel to the inch markers on the yardstick.

After you find you are able to execute this properly without a ball, try placing a ball about 5 inches from one end of the yardstick, and actually stroke it off the end of your improvised platform. If you are executing the stroke properly, the ball will roll off the end of the yardstick. You can gradually move the ball further from the end of the stick. The longer you can keep the ball on its "track," the truer will be your stroke.

This picture is a representation of three concentric 15-foot circles, 15, 30 and 45 feet from the cup. In making a general survey of the green, I imagine these three circles in order to determine what type of putting stroke I will have to utilize. If my ball lies within the closest circle, I will use a putting stroke that involves hand action alone; if it lies within the 30-foot circle, I will use a stroke involving hand and forearm action; if it lies within the 45-foot circle, I will use a stroke involving hand, arm, and shoulder action.

I also use these imaginary circles to help me picture the track of the ball in the longer putts, especially on undulating greens, where part of the ball's track may run uphill or sidehill and another part level or reverse sidehill.

The Fundamentals of a Good Putting Stroke

A view of the three 15-foot circles which I use to gauge distance, imagine the track of the ball, and decide the strength of my stroke. I am practicing a backswing at the 45-foot distance. The blade is still "square" even though the backswing is necessarily longer than for a 30-footer or a 15-footer. At the 45-foot distance there is some shoulder action, as well as hand and arm action. My stance is a little wider than at the shorter distances, and I have allowed for more freedom in my stroke.

Here is a front view of the same 45-foot putt. You will understand now what I mentioned earlier on page 50 concerning the exaggerated lowness of the backstroke. The putting blade does come off the turf, however slightly, yet it constantly remains in "square-blade position." The "hooding" action of the left wrist is particularly evident in this illustration.

The Fundamentals of a Good Putting Stroke

Here are two views of a 30-foot putt. The backswing is slightly longer at this distance than that used at distances of 15 feet and under. Note how low and close to the green the blade is and how it still maintains its "squareness to the line." At this distance, I am using a stroke with both hand and arm action in it. By this technique I can get more power and freedom than I would need for a shorter putt.

These are views of a 15-foot putt. At this distance, the golfer's stroke is altogether more compact—the feet are a little closer together and the upper part of the right arm hugs the body a little more. The entire emphasis is on a shorter, sharper, and firmer stroke. This is especially true of the left hand, whose firmness must prevent the right hand from twisting the club out of line at the point of impact. At distances of 15 feet and closer, the putting stroke consists primarily of hand action. Remember that at all distances the left hand and wrist should "hood" the face of the club during the backswing in order to keep it constantly perpendicular to the line of the putt. Once again, this picture illustrates how low and level to the turf the blade should remain.

None of the pictures were posed at "stop" position. All of these putts were actually stroked.

Equipment

Getting the ball into the cup after it has reached the green is one of golf's greatest problems, and the stroke by which this act is accomplished differs radically from every other stroke in the game.
CHICK EVANS

LIKE LITTLE BOYS and girls, putters come in a wide variety of sizes, shapes, and weights. And we all have our favorites, both among boys and girls and among putters. Basically, putters can be classified either as blade putters or mallet-type putters. There are a great many oddities in the construction of putters—goose-neck shafts, bent shafts, odd heads and other variations—but on the whole, for our purposes we need only talk about blade and mallet putters.

Regarding your putter's length, I will only say that your putter should be as long or as short as you want it to be, as long as you are comfortable using it. I have seen very tall men with little short-shafted putters and short men with long-shafted putters. I have indicated the necessity of "sitting down" a bit to the ball and the importance of having your head and eyes directly over the ball when it is placed off your left foot. Your own physique, height and arm length will guide you to a general selection of a putter that "fits" you in length.

After that, you will have to experiment with perhaps ten, perhaps a hundred, putters before you will find the one that feels good to you—the one that will inspire your confidence to the point where when you miss a "makeable" putt you will accuse yourself and not the putter.

Try various weights of blade putters first. You will find that the heavier the head is, the less delicate your touch will be. A heavy putter feels "powerful," but remember that it may be hard to control on a slick green. Try a very light putter and you will soon discover that it takes a real "hit" to hole a 3- or 4-footer. And you may not have the courage to hit it hard enough. You will probably decide on a medium-weight club, thus compromising between "touch" and "power."

There are various angles of inclination between putter head and shaft. Some are more "upright" than others, in that the shaft is inserted into the putter head closer to an absolute right angle, like the relationship of the shaft to the club head in a croquet mallet. Theoretically, the more upright your putter shaft is the closer you can approach a true pendulum action in swinging the blade. However, since you will be slightly in back of the ball when you apply the energy to swing the putter blade back and forth you will need some angle in your shaft in order to be comfortable. You will also have to consider carefully the amount of "loft" in the face of your putter. I personally prefer a blade putter of the "Cash-in" type because it has nice parallel lines at the front of the face and at the back, which, I feel, help me line up my right angles. I also like to inscribe my putter with a black line at the "sweet spot." This becomes my putting line because it is parallel to the line of my putt and at a right angle to the face of the blade.

These days, many putters are made with little or no loft, in contrast to the old days when putter blades were made at almost the same angles as a No. 2 iron. They used to be called "putting cleeks." I believe that it was the realization that the ball should be given an end-over-end roll, and that the lofted blades caused the ball to hop for a foot or two before settling down to a steady roll, that caused the trend away from lofted putters. The development of fine, smoothly cut greens also helped to bring about the change.

Experiment with putters of various lofts until you find one that enables you to roll the ball best. A variation of a fraction of an inch in the placement of the ball relative to the imaginary line that extends from the inner edge of your left shoe will change the angle at which your putter blade meets the ball. If you tend to play the ball back toward the center of your stance and find your hands in front of the ball at the moment of impact, and if you are using a putter with little or no loft, you may discover that you have a "negative" loft and are striking a descending and therefore unwelcome blow. In such a case, you probably should use a putter with a little loft.

The various shaft resiliencies will affect your decision concerning your putter. My putter shaft has a little "give" to it and gives off a decided metallic "ping" when I hit the ball "on" the "sweet spot." If you can find a putter that feels good in every respect, buy it by all

Equipment

means and stick with it for a while, or at least long enough to give the club a chance to prove itself to you.

I know several good putters who have never changed their putters in years and years of play. On the other hand, I know even more good putters who have many different types and are constantly changing from one to another. A good deal of the battle is psychological, and if you think that by changing to a new putter you will have more success, do so, but if you can stick with one for years, as so many good putters do, I sincerely believe you will be better off. For usually, the fault lies not in the club but in the man "wielding the stick."

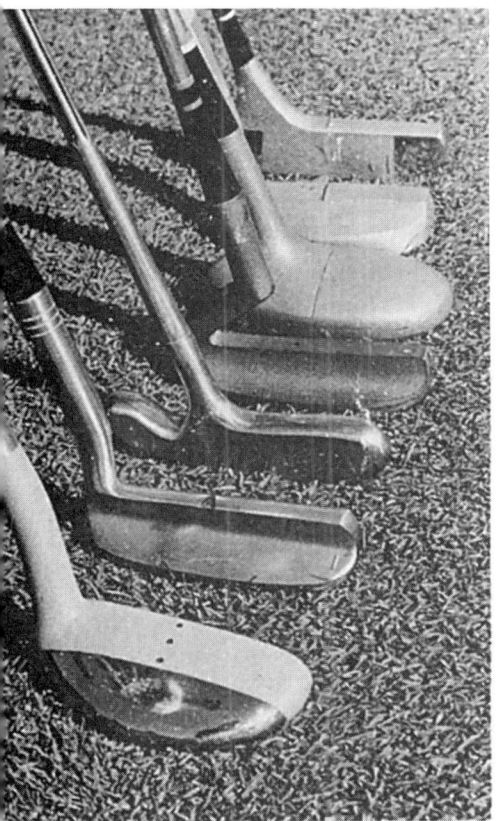 

Here are two views of seven different types of putters. Note the difference between the mallet-type putters and the blade-type putters.

The Etiquette of Putting

You're a good loser if you can grip the winner's hand without wishing it was his throat.

HAL CHADWICK

THE ETIQUETTE OF putting is based upon long-established rules of golf and everyday common-sense politeness. As you well know, the player whose ball lies farthest away from the pin is expected to play first toward the hole. That player has the right to ask you to remove your ball if it lies near or on his anticipated line to the hole. So it is most polite for each golfer to be aware of the fact that his ball may interfere with another player's line. Without being asked by the other player to do so, he should, once he reaches the green, promptly proceed to mark his ball in the approved fashion.

The rules of golf provide that if a player wishes to "mark" his ball he should place a small coin, preferably a dime or penny, immediately behind it. If the coin itself should prove to be an impediment or even a distraction, the player should ask, "Would you like me to mark my ball above or below the line?" The coin should then be placed one or two putter-head lengths away from the original position of the ball, above or below the line of the other player's putt, depending on the player's preference, and in a spot which is least apt to provide interference with the other player.

The player should also be alert for situations in which another player is about to chip for the pin or play out of a trap and the player's own ball lies close to the pin, where it might stop the other player's ball should it roll toward the cup. In such a situation merely ask, "Do you want me to mark my ball?" Sometimes you may be surprised to find that your opponent does want you to mark the ball. On the whole, the best policy is to be aware of possible infringement on another player's line and to ask the polite question, "Shall I mark it or not?"

Once you have made your first putt up close to the pin, you should look to see whether or not your new "spot" now infringes on an opponent's line and should be prepared to mark your ball again. If the ball is quite close to the cup, be prepared to sink the short putt. When you do so, be extremely careful of your foot marks on the green. Walk around to the "back of the hole" or the side opposite

The Etiquette of Putting 69

the one your opponent will be playing from when you mark your ball, lean over carefully taking care not to use your putter as a crutch or cane, for this is an easy way to damage the surface of the green. Also avoid ruffling the surface of the green by turning your spikes. Remember that your opponent may overrun the cup and be inconvenienced by a torn-up green on his next putt as a result of your carelessness in marking your ball.

Another point of putting etiquette: You should be aware of the possible "borrow" which will be required for your opponent's putt line and should refrain from interfering with the "borrow" line in any way. Avoid casting your shadow on it; avoid standing in line with it; in fact, avoid standing at any spot where you might be a distraction to your opponent as he prepares to putt.

You should be careful not to move until your opponent has putted his ball. You should also make sure not to jingle change in your pocket. Even the movement of your caddy on his way to the next tee can be disturbing. Caddies should be well instructed by their caddy-masters, and their instructions should be enforced by the intelligent player so that no "outside" noise or movement spoils the golf game on the green.

A further point of etiquette that is sometimes unintentionally violated by the golfer: When you have holed a putt under circumstances which your opponent also faces, don't say, for example, "Boy, am I glad to get that one down. That green is really slippery." Without realizing it, you have placed a mental obstruction in the mind of the second golfer, who must still attempt to hole his putt.

It is considered polite to remove your ball from the cup once you have holed it. Sometimes you may even find it convenient and polite to retrieve your opponent's ball from the cup after he has holed a "long one." When you pick the ball out for him, it is polite to smile, too, no matter how hard it may be!

Although I am fully aware that no putt should be conceded, I am also practical enough to realize that the normal play at your country club will be lengthened another half-hour if everyone is forced to sink even his 4-inch putts. Putts are conceded in many foursomes and I firmly believe that the reason for many concessions lies in a fear on the part of the player making the concession that he may be required to sink a putt of similar distance if he does not "concede" the nasty 3-footer.

Putts longer than a foot should not be conceded. You should plan to sink all your second putts and not wait for a concession. Don't ever ask, "Gimme this one?" for you lay yourself wide open to your opponent, who no matter how friendly he may be, need only say, "No, I think I'll let you miss that one!" and you usually will too!

On the other hand, when your opponent says, "You can have that!" by all means walk right to your ball, reach down, and pick it up without further ado. Don't stop to putt it in spite of the concession, because half the time you'll miss it through inattention or carelessness. Then you will feel guilty about taking the 5 that you know in your heart might have been or should have been a 6.

Occasionally a situation arises where two balls are apparently the same distance away from the cup and are lying on divergent bearings, so that it is difficult to determine which ball is away without actually measuring their relative distances. Theoretically, the distances should be measured and in the case of tournament play they would be. But in the usual friendly match, the one who is "away" is usually determined either by the golfers themselves or, in case of doubt, by a caddie standing at the pin, in a position to get a better perspective of the distance to each ball.

In such a case, I make it a general practice to putt first. Quite often I see two players in this situation each saying to the other "You're away," as if each were afraid to putt. From my own experience, I feel that the player who says, "I'll putt first," and then does so, has a distinct advantage. I prefer to putt first because I am usually confident that I will sink my putt and will thus force my opponent to sink his putt in order to stay even with me.

Another advantage to putting first is that you will not feel yourself rushed while studying your putt. Thus, you will take your time and putt your very best. On the other hand, by delaying your putt you may find that the player who putts first takes a little more time than you think necessary, causes you to become impatient, and even causes you to rush your putt. This is especially true on a crowded course. By the same token, it is a very impolite practice to take so much time for your own putt that you infringe on the other player's time and opportunity to make a studied putt of his own.

If you have been an "after you, dear Gaston" type of putter up until now, I would suggest that you now change your attitude to a more positive one and adopt my "putt-first-when-you-can" psychology. It works for me, I can assure you.

The Strategy of Putting

A missed putt of only 30½ inches on the final hole of the playoff with Lew Worsham proved fatal to Sam Snead in the 1947 Open Championship at the St. Louis (Mo.) Country Club.

Snead failed on his short putt and then watched as Worsham sank his from 29½ inches for the title. Had Snead gotten the putt down, he would have kept the playoff alive. Instead he lost 69-70.

All even coming to the final green, Worsham was 40 feet from the flag on the apron in two while Snead was 15 feet away on the green. Worsham chipped so well he lipped the cup. Snead's first putt stopped short. . . .

Assuming he was still out, Snead walked up to stroke his seemingly short putt but Worsham evidently felt he might be away and asked for a measurement. The tape showed the exact distance and Snead moved up to putt again. His line was off, however, and his ball lipped the cup and stayed out. Worsham then stepped up and dropped his all-important putt for victory.

HERBERT WARREN WIND

WHILE THE WORD "strategy" may suggest connivance in trying to get the better of an opponent, this is not really the case. Since golf is a game played by gentlemen (and gentlewomen), one never takes unfair advantage of an opponent anywhere on the golf course.

However, it is necessary that every golfer understand some of the factors involved in the strategy of putting so that he will better understand his rights and obligations on the green, both within and beyond the rules of golf.

As I have already pointed out, the person whose ball lies farthest away from the cup has the obligation and right to play for the cup before anyone else. Sometimes it will happen that one player is in a trap alongside a green, say 25 feet from the hole, while another player or opponent has his ball on the green but may be 30 or 40 feet away from the pin. The first impulse of the golfer in the trap is to play out of the trap without considering the fact that his opponent is in fact "away" from the pin. Thus, one of the first strategic factors to consider is the effect of playing in one's true "turn."

Let's suppose that both you and your opponent have taken 3 strokes on a 5-par hole. Your ball is in the trap 25 feet away and his is on the green 35 feet away. If you proceed to play out of the trap before he makes his first putt, you are going to give him a certain advantage, no matter what the results of your turn may be. If you miss your trap shot and your ball remains in the trap, you immediately make him aware of the fact that he can probably 2-putt for a win and 3-putt for a tie, because at best you will be on the green on your fourth shot while he will still be lying 3. Now, suppose you don't miss your trap shot but put it up "stoney" 3 feet away for a possible 5 on the hole. Your opponent then knows that he *must* 2-putt. He will try that much harder to be careful not to take more than two putts.

Now, let's consider the alternative strategy of waiting your turn and asking your opponent to putt first before you play out of the trap. First of all, your suggestion may come to him as a rather disturbing surprise. He has walked up to the green and very enjoyably contemplated what you are going to do with your trap shot. He's hoping you will miss it and give him an easy win on the hole. He probably hasn't measured the distances from the pin to determine that he is in fact "away" by a few feet.

When you tell him to putt first before you play from the bunker, which you can and should do, you can see that his normal routine is going to be shaken a little bit. As he is apt to hurry his survey and his putt, he has a good chance of either putting short or charging by the cup in an effort to be sure and be "up" to the cup.

After he putts, your situation in the trap will seem much clearer, and you will now have the advantage that you were about to hand him on a silver platter. If he has putted badly and left himself an awkward second putt you will have that much more motivation to get your trap shot very close to the pin. If you get your ball even closer to the pin than his ball is, you will make him putt his second putt before you try for your par.

Even if your strategy does not work and your opponent putts dead on his first putt and gets his par, you still have obtained a psychological advantage over him. A golfer can "take" just so many "pressure putts," and that long first putt which he wasn't expecting to have to make can be classed as a "pressure putt." After a number of such "pressure putts," the best golfer is bound to break down and miss a short one sooner or later.

Another advantage to putting second is that you can watch how

The Strategy of Putting 73

other balls roll near the cup. If you are on the green and your opponent is off, watch the way his ball travels over the green in order to determine the speed of the green. Be especially careful to watch for unusual rolls around or near the cup.

No matter in what order you are putting, always watch what happens to your own ball as it travels past the cup, for the line it takes, even if it goes several feet past the cup, will almost approximate the line it will have to retrace in coming back to the cup. So often I see the average golfer start to groan and complain when his putt races unexpectedly past the hole. Instead of thinking, "What an awful putt that was!" and diverting his attention thereby, he should be watching the action of the ball closely and laying the foundation of knowledge he will need for the second putt. It is equally true that you may get "local knowledge" from the behavior of your opponent's ball around the cup. Always be ready to get any possible information you can from the other player. It is free and often very valuable.

I have remarked earlier that, if possible, you should never give "consolation to the enemy" by putting first when you do not have to. Searching for an apt illustration of why you should never concede a putt to an opponent, there came to mind the classic story of the Al Watrous–Bobby Cruickshank match in the P.G.A. Championship of 1932. Dawson Taylor and I are both good friends of Al Watrous, the long-time pro at the famous Oakland Hills Country Club, which ranks with the Oakmont Country Club in Pittsburgh, among the most difficult tests of golf in the country. So I suggested that Al tell us the story of his "infamous" conceded putt in '32. Here is the story in his own words.

"Well, it was a third-round match at thirty-six holes at the Keller course in St. Paul, Minnesota, and I had played the morning round very well—about 5 under par, in fact, although since it was match play, not all the putts were holed. I had built up a satisfying lead of 5 up at the end of the first eighteen holes of the afternoon round, and I had increased my lead to 9 up with only thirteen to play. The sixth hole is a short par 3, about 165 yards long, and Bobby missed the green. I hit the corner of the green with my tee shot. Bobby chipped by the cup about 6 feet above the hole. I putted up close and Bobby conceded my second putt for a 3.

"A little bit earlier, Bobby had mentioned to me that 'this was the worst beating he had ever had, and, since I was 9 up at the time, I would be going 10 up if he missed the putt. Feeling a bit sorry for him and not wanting to see him go down in double figures, I conceded him the putt. I can remember so clearly that as we walked off the green to the next tee, an elevated one, we passed a man who had been lying on the bank of the tee, looking down at the sixth green, and observing the play and the conceded putt.

"As I went by him, I heard him say to another person near him, 'He shouldn't have done that! He might be sorry for that!' I certainly heard it. Whether Bobby did, I don't know. Perhaps he did, too.

"Anyway, I was still 9 up and playing the seventh hole with only twelve to go. Bobby holed a 20-foot putt for a birdie at the seventh while I missed an 8-footer. I was then 8 up. The next hole has a big tree in the center and I pushed my tee shot to the right and had to take a 9 iron to get over the tree. I got over the tree all right but I was short of the green. Bobby got on in 2, won with a par and was 7 down.

"The ninth hole is a long 4-par and we were both on in 2. I was away and 3-putted while Bobby took 2 putts and was only 6 down.

"I still remember the change in attitude of both of us as we went to the tenth tee. Earlier we had been discussing Bobby's chances of getting a job in one of the Detroit district courses and how I could help him.

"Suddenly, Bobby was all business and the friendliness went out the window. He could sense that he was back in the match.

"I won't tell you what happened, hole by hole, because for me it was simply disastrous. I played well but Bobby played, and particularly putted, sensationally. On 18 straight holes after the famous conceded putt, Bobby had 11 1-putts. One of them was a 70-footer on the fifteenth. Another hole we halved in birdies. But coming to the eighteenth I was still 1 up and Bobby had played the back nine in 6 under par. He knocked in another long putt for a birdie at eighteen. We were in overtime and the big lead I had had was all gone.

"The first, second, and third extra holes were tied, although twice I had the chance to roll in the winning putt. The story of the fourth extra hole, I think, is funny enough, looking back at it now, to retell in more detail.

"The fourth hole at Keller is a short hole, probably about 140 yards. Bobby drove his tee shot over the green and up a bank behind it.

"I hit my tee shot 2 feet from the hole. Cruickshank putted down the hill and was still outside of my ball in 2. He putted again, and missed, and was outside of me in 3. Bobby was definitely in for a 4 at least, and I hadn't taken my second shot yet. He was just about to shake hands with me but decided not to and knocked his putt in for the 4. My putt was a delicate downhill putt on a very close-shaven green and I didn't want to leave it short. I didn't. It went past the hole not more than a foot. I thought Bobby was going to concede my putt, but he didn't and I proceeded to putt my 1-footer too delicately. There was nap or grain in the green and it caused my ball to veer off and miss the cup. If I had hit the putt more firmly I would have canceled the effect of the grain and probably would have holed it. Needless to say, we had tied in bogey 4's. I had three-putted from 2 feet away.

"The next hole was the last in the overtime. Bobby holed another 6-footer, making his par. I was on the green in 2, putted too strongly, went by the cup and missed a 3-footer coming back. Cruickshank had won an 'impossible-to-win' match. My advice to you is, 'Don't ever concede your opponent a putt—*not even a 2-incher!*' "

Scoring Your Putts

After one of the greatest putting exhibitions ever seen on any golf course, Horton Smith, angular Chicago professional, today edged his fellow townsman, Harry Cooper, out of what appeared to be certain victory in the Masters Tournament at the Augusta National Golf Club. . . .

Smith holed a 43-footer on the 68th, an 8-footer on the 69th and a 16-footer on the 71st.
NEWS ITEM: AUGUSTA, GEORGIA. APRIL 16, 1936.

MANY GOLFERS KEEP an accurate record of the number of times they break 100, 90, or 80, but very few do I see keeping track of the number of putts they used each round. It is obvious that out of the 72 strokes it takes to shoot a par round of golf, 36 strokes must be putts, and that is allowing only two putts per hole. If you consider the variety of woods and irons needed to make the other 36 strokes, you begin to realize the importance of good putting. It is literally "a game within a game."

Champion golfers of today consistently report eighteen-hole totals of 27 or fewer putts. This means that on eight or nine greens the player has gotten down in a single putt. And often these rounds are not "par-breakers," but just "par-savers."

While we cannot all hope to achieve the putting proficiency of a Rosburg or a Casper, we can all make the effort to improve our putting ability to the extent of saving at least one stroke per round. It is my considered opinion that with the practice methods and an understanding of the theories in this book, you can save several strokes per round in your future golf games.

One thing you can do is start measuring your putting ability. That ability can be measured from one game to the next, both in terms of the total number of putts taken and the total footage of your "one-

Scoring Your Putts

putts." Here is an example of a scorecard which keeps track of your putts as well as your total score:

Par	Score	Putts	Footage	Par	Score	Putts	Footage
4	5	2		4	4	1	6'
5	6	2		3	4	2	
3	4	1	6'	4	5	2	
4	5	2		4	5	2	
4	4	2		5	5	1	4'
4	5	2		3	4	(3)	
3	3	1	10'	4	6	2	
4	4	1	15'	5	5	1	12'
4	5	2		4	5	2	
35	41	15	31'	36	43	16	22'
				71	84	31	53'

If you had played this round, you could afterwards make a note of the 3-putt green and analyze why this minor disaster occurred. You might also be surprised to discover that if it hadn't been for the six 1-putt greens, your score would have soared from a respectable 84 to an even 90.

Take my advice and, starting with your next game, keep a tally of your total putts as well as the total footage of your 1-putts. Then you can keep a record of your putting ability from game to game. You can also watch the effect of your improvement on your total score. As Lloyd Mangrum is reported to have said when someone criticized his stroke, "Are we playing 'how' or 'how many'?"

The Survey

Par allows us 2 putts to the green; 36 to the round. But who is it plants the proper shot on the green steadily, for even one round? So far as memory serves, I have never seen it done. Somewhere I have heard that championship golf, round after round, averages 32 putts. This means that on at least four greens the player has got down in a single putt. And in most instances, that putt resulted from an accurate chip, taking up the slack of a bigger shot which just failed of its aim.
ROBERT T. JONES, JR.

YOU HAVE UNDOUBTEDLY heard the expression "reading the greens." I feel that the more general heading "survey" better suggests what must be done to understand the various factors that will affect a given putt.

I believe that the average golfer plays from 90 to 95 per cent of his golf on his "home" course, whether it is private or public. Therefore, it is my suggestion that since you do play so often over one particular course, it would be wise for you to analyze carefully your own greens and their particular characteristics. Once you have a greater knowledge of them, you will be able to putt on them more successfully.

To give you an idea of how to perform a "survey," let us first consider all the greens on a particular course. For you it will be an imaginary one, but for practical purposes I will have in mind the greens of the Detroit Golf Club. First, what "speed" would you classify these greens? I would answer, "medium speed"—neither extremely fast or hard, nor extremely slow and soft. Second, what general contour do you find? Do they slope one way or the other? In general, the greens that I have in mind slope gently from back to front and have easy, large rolls in them. There are several examples of plateau-type greens. Are any of the greens any faster than the others? Yes, several that are shaded by the large oak trees have a slightly different type of grass and substructure and are therefore harder under foot and faster than the "normal" green.

The Survey

What about the position of the pins? Especially on the pleateau-type greens, when the pins are actually placed on the plateaus, the difficulty of an approach putt is increased immeasurably. Also, on the several greens which have long "humps" or ripples in them, if the approach putt must go over the mound or ridge, the predicament is much more difficult.

With this type of general analysis of the greens that he must play, the intelligent player can begin to plan his strategy before he even steps on the first tee.

The golfer is quite often able to see from the tee itself approximately where the pin is placed on a particular green. Although this is not usually possible on the long 4-par or 5-par holes, it is possible to see the location of the pin on the green on about half the holes.

Let me take you to the fifth hole at the Detroit Golf Club so that I can illustrate the meaning of "survey" and "reading the greens." This hole is a long 4-par (440 yards) through a tree-lined fairway to an elevated plateau type of green. The average golfer cannot make this green in 2, so he will be chipping from, say, the edge of the green or from perhaps 25 or more yards away.

Today, the pin is on the plateau at the back of the green. This means that it will be best to be strong with your approach, if possible, so as to get up onto the plateau. Now, as we come up the hill in front of the green, let us look more carefully at the placement of the pin and the slope of the green. Our closer observation shows that the pin is on the left side of the plateau and that the green definitely slopes downward from the right to left toward the cup. With this information stored in our memory we proceed to play the chip shot firmly onto the plateau. Since as a general rule a right-to-left roll is more favorable for the average right-handed golfer, we have tried to favor the right side of this cup, hoping, of course, to chip right in, but expecting to be anywhere from 3 to 15 feet away, depending upon our golfing ability.

The important thing is that we have tried to be aware of the particular characteristics of the green from the moment we teed off, instead of simply and haphazardly aiming for the pin and avoiding until too late the solution to the problems presented by the green.

We frequently hear of a golfer having a sensational round of putting, in which he needed only 25 putts for eighteen holes and scored eleven 1-putts. Often such a round is more the result of accurate planning than of outstanding putting.

THE GENERAL SURVEY FROM OFF THE GREEN

This brings to mind a round that I had in the Masters at Augusta, Georgia, a few years ago. On the 72-par course I scored a 70; yet I hit only nine greens in par figures! Why did I break par? Because I needed only 27 putts in the whole round. The total footage of my 1-putt greens was 60 feet. I did hole putts of 20, 15, and 10 feet, but the remainder were for the most part short putts. These short putts resulted from accurate chipping and approach shots.

According to my method of analysis, this was not an exceptional round of putting. I would describe it more as a round of steady putting, combined with fine chipping which placed the ball near the hole often enough to get me in with a single putt.

On this same round, my playing partner, a very good hitter, shot a 79, although he hit fifteen greens in par figures. He complained to me about his "poor putting," but I tried to console him by pointing out to him that considering the large and undulating greens of the course, his scoring difficulty was due more to faulty planning than to faulty putting.

Our play on the eighteenth hole illustrates the point very well. The cup was cut on the lower level of a big terraced green. I had already

The Survey

analyzed the eighteenth hole while we were playing off the adjacent tenth tee. I had stored the data in my memory and had resolved to play my second shot of the eighteenth on the short side of the hole, so that I would be able to play up to the hole instead of facing the problem of negotiating a tricky downhill putt. Actually I played the shot a little too cautiously and left my ball a yard short of the green. Still, I faced a relatively simple straight-uphill chip to the cup. My partner, on the other hand, hit a straight, bold second shot which carried over the flagstick and ended up on the upper level, 60 feet from the hole. He faced a treacherous downhill and sidehill approach putt—much more difficult than mine, even though my ball was off the green and his was on. He didn't "borrow" quite enough, and he also misjudged the speed of the green slightly. He found himself about 9 feet from the hole. He 3-putted for a bogey while I chipped my relatively straight-uphill shot to within 18 inches of the cup for a par.

I would put the blame for the bogey on my partner's second shot rather than his putting. While he hit that second shot well, the strategy called for a safer shot short of the hole rather than a bold shot "long." While it is difficult for a player to play for position and for safety at the same time, there are many occasions when it is worth the gamble to play the shot to a position where the succeeding shot will be easier. Always remember that all your shots to the green are going to play a factor in the ease or difficulty of putting.

Imagination

British Open, 1924.

At the eighteenth I was confident I had victory in the palm of my hand, for here was a short par-4 hole with the wind at my back. I got a long tee shot, some 300 yards, leaving me a short seven-iron for my second. Again a series of traps crossed the front of the green. However, they didn't seem to be too troublesome considering the shortness of the shot I had to make.

I played my second shot too boldly and went past the flag to the back edge of the green. Here I was on this fast green . . . on the back edge at that . . . and I needed to get down in two. I putted down, sloping away, and left myself five feet short. Had I hit it a tiny bit harder I would have rolled almost to the hole. But a semicircular ridge held my ball and left me with a most difficult putt.

With such a fast green I knew my stroke must be delicate. I looked over both sides of the hole. There was a slim chance of a slight roll as it went down a little incline toward the hole. I studied it carefully once more. I decided there was a double roll to the left the last two feet. I stood and set myself with one thing uppermost in mind. I must hit the ball delicately. And in a situation like this delicacy is difficult due to the extreme nervous tension one is under. But then I had a second thought which helped greatly in my executing the shot correctly and in not being overanxious to see where the ball was going. Should I miss, I'd only need to stay over another day to beat Whitcombe in the playoff of the British Championship. If I holed, I became the British Open Champion.

While ten thousand people held their breath, I stroked the ball . . . gently but firmly; it righted the last turn, straightened out and headed for home! I threw my putter into the air and never saw the ball or the putter again. But I sure saw that British Open trophy.

WALTER HAGEN

A MOST IMPORTANT factor in your survey is your imagination—your ability to picture in your mind the track of the ball up a hill or down a hill, over a roll or up onto a plateau. In very difficult situations, it is sometimes necessary for you to call upon all your experience and, as I will point out in my discussion of "overallowance" in the amount of "borrow," you will occasionally disregard what your

Imagination

eyes seem to tell you and act upon your intelligence and your experience.

Also connected with the use of your imagination is the factor of strategy—whether to "go for" the putt or settle for a 2-putt and be satisfied. "Experience is the best teacher," as we all know, but many times I have seen good golfers, who, in spite of their experience, fail to imagine the consequences and therefore act upon false premises in trying to sink putts when good judgment would have told them not to try.

I have particularly in mind the very slippery eighteenth green at the Meadowbrook Country Club in Northville, just outside of Detroit, the site of many Motor City Open Golf Tournaments. There is a large step in the middle of this green running almost directly across from right to left about one-third of the way back from the front edge. If the pin is placed at the foot of the slope, that is, on the front part of the green, and the player's second shot is strong and his ball climbs the slope above the hole, it is practically impossible to hole the putt, especially if the situation is complicated by a sharp break either to the right or the left. Yet, many times I have seen experienced professionals, with what I would say is one chance in a hundred, attempt to hole their putts from above the cup, drift 4 feet beyond it, and then miss the return putt, instead of using their imagination to visualize a dying ball almost stopping a couple of feet above the cup and then slowly continuing down the slope, inch by inch, to a safe 6 inches or so from the hole. Such a move would guarantee a safe 2-putt without eliminating the "long shot" of sinking the first putt.

So, practice picturing what your ball will do while going up a slope with a strong break to the cup. An imaginary conversation with yourself might go something like this: "It will be going up the slope, so I'll have to hit it a little bit harder than would appear necessary, and because of the slope left I'd better play it about a foot above the cup. No, I won't either. I'll play it a foot and a half above the cup, because it will be dying at the cup and therefore breaking more. Perhaps I can find a 'spot' above the cup to aim for. Yes, there's a blade of clover about 14 inches above the cup. I'll pretend the cup is 4 inches to the right of that clover and plan to stop right on it. Now, remember, firm grip because you're going uphill." And thus your imagination and the sum of your previous putting experience help you to solve each problem and become a better putter, day by day.

The Routine of Putting

The greatest five [putters], in my book, are Walter J. Travis, Jerry Travers, Bob Jones, Walter Hagen and Horton Smith.
                                                    GRANTLAND RICE

WE HAVE ALREADY discussed how you should survey the green as you approach it from a distance. You have formed your general impression of its character, decided whether it is fast or slow, and radically uphill or downhill, and taken into consideration the mound or plateau you must traverse to success. Now, let us get into what I call the "routine of putting"—the actions the golfer goes through immedately before he strokes the ball.

We have all watched the top professional golfers undertaking their putting surveys and their routine preliminary actions preparatory to putting. Each one of us should adopt a set routine, and once it has been established, we should make it a habit and act it out invariably each time we putt.

I will describe my own routine as a typical example. First, if I possibly can, I try to get a view of the green from a position level with the ball while it is lying on the green. This can only be done when the green is elevated enough to permit one to get on a slope directly in front of or directly behind the ball.

If this is not possible, I take my putter in my left hand and squat down behind the ball in line with the pin and attempt to determine the "line" of the putt. I then move to the middle of the "down" side at a point halfway between the cup and the ball, so that the ball, the cup, and my body form an equilateral triangle. From this point I determine the distance of the putt, as I will describe in the next chapter.

Sometimes this "routine" is shortened if I am able both to watch while another player putts first and to stand in my measuring spot without interfering with either his vision or his line. I can then determine the distance of the putt, just how hard I will hit this particu-

The Routine of Putting 85

lar putt, and whether I will "go for" the cup or, if the green is particularly slippery, "play it safe" and "lag it up." At this point I am already making imaginary strokes with my putter.

I am now about ready to step up to the ball and assume my putting stance. I begin by taking up a "last-gasp" position several steps behind the ball so that I can confirm my earlier decision as to the "line." I try to avoid changing my mind at this point. I believe that second-guessing yourself is a very serious mistake. It should be avoided, because it undermines your confidence. No one can consistently "read the greens" with 100 per cent accuracy, so be satisfied to do your best, on the basis of your original decision.

As I said, I now have my hands in their putting grip, but my grip is extremely loose so that I can more readily "feel" the clubhead as I make little strokes a foot or so away from the ball. Next, I step into my putting stance, placing the left foot first, and check the line off the inner sole of my left shoe for ball placement. Then I aim my left elbow at right angles to the line of the putt. I am breathing deeply and slowly. I have lined up my putter blade so that it is "square to the line." I am concentrating on holding my head steady. My head and eyes are directly over the ball. I take a deep breath, holding it, and am ready to "take off" in my backswing and stroke the ball in its end-over-end roll into the cup.

I am not saying that you must do any or all of the steps that I do. There are variations of all kinds, but all good putters use some of these techniques, and others have even more elaborate preparations for their putts. I wish I could go along with Bobby Cruickshank and his "miss-'em-quick" philosophy. It is against my nature—yet, I would advise you not to be too slow or too complicated in your preliminary routine.

I do not believe in looking a putt over from both in back and in front of the cup unless it appears to be a particularly treacherous one—like the double-roll variety. I think that an adequate and less confusing "study" can be accomplished from the ball's side of the cup, and that too long or varied a study will only lead to confusion and indecision.

Do not allow yourself to be distracted once you have assumed your putting stance and are preparing to stroke the ball. I'll agree that this is, at times, difficult, especially for the professional golfer in tournament play, who has to contend with a gallery that often moves in the player's line of vision, or for the amateur on the ninth or eighteenth hole, where there may be people waiting to start play or just watching. At any rate, you should try to be aware of outside distractions as you prepare to putt. For example, if you happen to catch sight of a caddy moving to the next tee and it interferes with your concentration, don't be afraid to relax your grip, straighten up, and even step away from the ball. Then repeat your final preliminaries after the distraction has passed. You will find that if you do this, you will approach the execution of your putt with much more confidence and relaxation, whereas, if you don't interrupt your preparations and merely proceed to putt in spite of the distracting influence, more often than not you will miss the putt.

Whether or not you prefer to place your putter blade in front of your ball before you get into your actual stroke is a matter of personal preference. Many good players do this. On the other hand, other good players prefer to begin from behind the ball in "square-blade" position. The reason for placing the blade in front of the ball is that some golfers believe they can visualize their "square-blade" position better without the putting line being blocked by a view of the ball. I believe that very little time should be wasted after the putter blade has been placed behind the ball and that the stroke should begin promptly, so as to allow no time for "tightening up" or "freezing" at the ball. If you find that you have difficulty deciding to "take off" into your backswing (and this happens to the best of golfers at some time or other in their careers), I recommend the following procedure to cure the trouble. First, put your blade in front of the ball in order to get the "square-blade" thought and alignment. Take as much time as you want to prepare your left elbow, ready your grip, relax your knees and visualize your line by swinging your head along the putting line from directly above the ball. Then start a "count-down." At the "3-2-1" count, place your putter behind the ball and immediately "take off" into your backswing.

There are famous golfers on the tournament trail who have been afflicted with the disease of "freezing" during the last several years. I wish I could get them to try my "cure" because I think it might help them to solve their problem once and for all.

Some further notes on routine: Since the golfer is now allowed to mark and clean his ball on the green without penalty (Rule 35-1d), I strongly advise that you take advantage of this recent liberalization of the rules of golf and carry a moist towel in your bag to aid you in cleaning your ball. There is something psychologically reassuring

The Routine of Putting

about knowing that your golf ball is perfectly clean and that it will not travel erratically as a result of any mud or sand on it. The present trend in golf-course design, and the much greater availability of water on the courses, have made the greens so much softer that often, especially in professional play, one sees the ball hit the green with such backspin that it tears out a good-sized divot.

The golfer is also now allowed "to repair damage to the putting green caused by the impact of a ball, but he may not step on the damaged area." There are small tools now available in the pro shops, much like a little spade, which are excellent for making ball-divot repairs. You should carry one with you constantly and be sure to repair not only your own divot marks but also those left by other careless golfers.

"Borrow" and "Break"

P.G.A. Record

Fewest Putts in an 18 Hole Round: 19, by Bill Nary in the 1952 Texas Open and by Bob Rosburg in the 1959 Pensacola Open.

"How much should I borrow?" "How far do you think this putt will break?" You will hear these expressions time and again as golfers seek advice from their partners or their caddies. So let's explain them with a few illustrations.

Think of steel balls in a pinball machine rolling up one slope and then down one side or the other. Or think of the banked corners around the Indianapolis Speedway, where the racers go high up into the corners and then come down into the straightaway. Or think of the way a boomerang sails out on a cushion of air and curves back so gracefully to the arms of the thrower: These are three illustrations of the same principle that makes a golf ball "borrow" and "break."

As you know already or will soon discover as you play golf and learn putting, many golf-course greens are "banked." Consequently, you will have to allow for the curving roll of the golf ball as it travels over their slopes. How much should you allow? Obviously, the more the "bank" or "tilt" of the green, the more the allowance for the alteration in the roll of the ball from a true, normal, straight path. As you play, experience will be your teacher. You will also find that for a long while you will tend to underestimate the amount of effect a banked slope will have on your ball.

Suppose you are contemplating a 20-foot putt on a green that is banked higher on the right than on the left. Obviously, you would have to hit this putt off to the right of a straight line between the ball and the cup. The degree to which you hit the ball to the right is the "borrow" from the right. The tendency of the ball to curve to the left is called its "break."

You "borrow" so many inches from the slope, but your putt "breaks" so many inches from the slope toward the cup. A green banked from right to left would naturally work in exactly the opposite fashion. That is, you would be "borrowing" from the slope on the left and your putt would be "breaking" to the right. I hope you are not completely confused, but that's the language of golf.

Tolerance for Error

I finally arrived at the conclusion which obtains as these lines are written; that the best system for me is to stroke the ball with as smooth a swing as I can manage, and try always to gauge an approach putt, or any putt except the short holing-out efforts, to reach the hole with a dying ball. Stewart Maiden had more than once urged this plan. "When the ball dies at the hole," said Stewart, "there are four doors; the ball can go in at the front, or the back, or at either side, wherever it touches the rim. But a ball that comes up to the hole with speed on it must hit the front door fairly in the middle; there are no side doors, and no Sunday entrance, for the putt that arrives under speed."

ROBERT T. JONES, JR.

IT IS MY FIRM conviction, based on years of my own experience, and on watching thousands of golfers attempt putts on a "borrowed" line, that 90 per cent are missed on the "low" side of the cup.

To explain more fully, the pictures on pages 90 and 91 show two views of a cup and pin on an inclined green. It is most evident that this pin slants to the left, away from a true perpendicular position, and, therefore, the practiced eye can see that the right-hand side of this cup (as you view it) is higher than the left, which is the "low" side. Now, not all cup placements are as evidently "off-angle" as this one is. Nevertheless, after seeing this example, I should like you from now on to pay special attention to the cups on your course, so that you may become an expert in finding the "high" side of the cup. It is very important that you do so.

Perhaps you have never seen a greens-keeper cut a fresh cup on your course. Well, he uses a tool that might be likened to a huge cookie-cutter to slice a circular cut into the ground, in order to remove a cylinder of turf about 10 inches long. He must necessarily pull this section out of the ground from directly above so as to have a perfectly level cup. Very rarely does the greens-keeper, much as he might try or wish to do so, actually remove the cut turf straight up. The result is, even on a supposedly level area, a cup with one side higher than the other.

When the cup has been cut from an area with a slight or even great slope in it, you will nearly always find the "high" side of that cup on the side toward the slope. This is very important for you to know,

THE "LOW" SIDE OF THE CUP

understand, and act upon. For when the ball is slowing down and is near the "high" side of the cup, it acts as though a magnet is there to draw it into the cup. I have seen this happen many times when it might appear that the ball is at least half an inch away from the lip of the cup and cannot possibly be expected to fall.

Now, let us go back to my first statement that 90 per cent of "borrowed" putts are missed on the low side of the cup. Suppose you are surveying a 10-foot putt with a right-to-left break or "borrow" of 6 inches. The photograph on page 92 indicates the normal track of this putt necessary to hole the ball in the exact center of the cup. But knowing two things about this situation changes your strategy for sinking this putt. First, your eye has informed you that the right side of the cup is the high side (this is also called "the pro side of the cup," for the obvious reason that the pros play for it all the time), and, therefore, this is the side you will aim for. Second, since you, and probably most golfers, are inclined to underestimate the amount

Tolerance for Error

THE "HIGH" SIDE OF THE CUP

On the "high" side of the cup it is difficult to make the ball stay out of the cup when you set it on the lip of the cup.

of roll on a "borrowed" putt, I suggest that you add an arbitrary 25 per cent to your original estimate of the required degree of "borrow." This gives you what I call "tolerance for error" or margin for error. By allowing this margin you can take advantage of the chance to enter the cup from the "high" side.

Remember, too, that the "dying ball" is much more affected by the contour of the green than a ball that is still moving from the power supplied by the putter. So why not make sure that the "dying ball" curves into the cup? Don't take my suggestion of a 25 per cent compensation too literally. It may be that your eye consistently overestimates the necessary roll or break. Only you can be the judge of that. In general, however, golfers tend to underestimate, so 25 per cent is generally sound.

When you are putting on the practice green you should experiment with various amounts of roll in the following fashion: Put down a ball 10 feet from the cup and arbitrarily figure the break. You

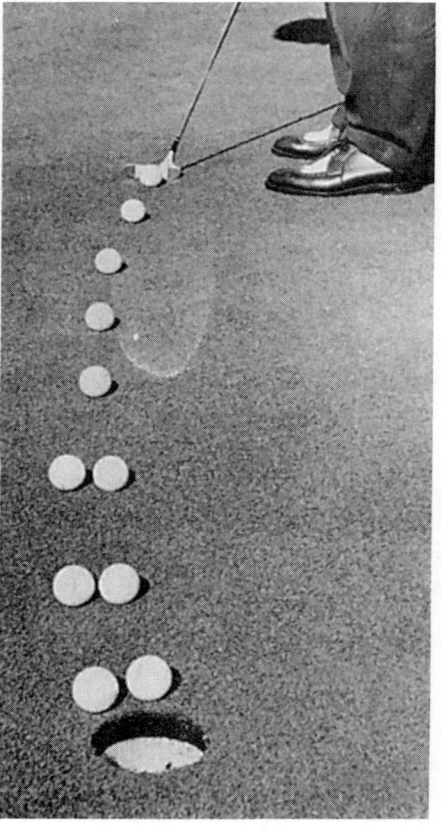

In the illustration on the left, the ball is stopping on the "low" side of the hole. On the right there are two tracks, one to the center of the cup and the other to the "high" side of the cup. Even if a putt to the "high" side is not hit hard enough, it often has enough power to get in either the center of the cup or the "low" side.

might, for example, figure the putt to break 4 inches right to left. Then place a tee 4 inches to the right of the cup and putt for the tee. Watch most carefully to be sure you are putting on the line 4 inches right of the cup. By experimenting with this system you will have a graphic illustration of the points I have been trying to make. After a while you can discard the tee and simply imagine the point toward which you are putting.

Another way to approach this problem is to decide that on right-to-left putts of lengths from 6 feet and up, you will arbitrarily open the blade a little bit more than your eye tells you to, and, in opposite fashion, on left-to-right putts of the same distance, close your blade slightly more than your eye tells you.

Whichever method works best you should adopt as a general rule and work at strenuously on the practice green until you have established your exact formula or percentage of overallowance. It is entirely possible that you will even wish to try this system on shorter putts.

You should also experiment with the ball position on borrowed putts. I find it more effective to have the ball slightly back toward the center of my stance on left-to-right putts and slightly in front of normal position on right-to-left putts. I feel that these variations in ball position are merely individual "margins for error" which help me to hit the ball on the line more often. Perhaps this method will help you too.

Measuring the Distance

Putting has won many a match for me. My penchant for holing the ball has made up for my wildness on the fairway in match after match. Much of the indifferent putting I have seen is due to the shaky, uncertain way a ball is hit. I like to hit a ball firmly. Banging the ball recklessly isn't going to help, of course, because mechanically it is as difficult to hole out from beyond the cup as it is from short of it, distances being equal. But, at least you've had one try when you go past the cup. There is a favorable psychology, as well as logic working for the player who consistently hits the ball hard enough to reach the hole. I've made it a point to note how often poor putters are short and I've been amazed at how much more frequently the good ones are beyond when they miss.

WALTER HAGEN

ORDINARILY, IT IS NOT possible for you to take out a tape measure and lay it down on the green between the hole and your ball to determine the distance between the ball and the hole. Nor are you allowed such a practice under the rules of golf. However, I strongly suggest that you get into the habit of measuring all your putt distances by any one of several methods. As a part of your general "survey" of the putt you should make it a practice to pace off the distance from your ball to the hole.

This need not be done too obviously. In my own case, I am certain that many of my opponents and fellow players are not even aware that I am mentally ticking off the number of paces I take toward the cup. Sometimes, when I have surveyed a putt from the opposite direction—from the other side of the pin—it is very simple to count my steps as I walk toward my ball and prepare to putt. When I actually pace toward the hole I count my paces up to within 3 steps of the hole. Since a normal pace equals about a yard, I then multiply the total number of paces by three and add the last 9 feet. I then have the approximate footage.

One reason that I measure is purely psychological. I usually don't announce it to the other players, but I like to think to myself as I

Measuring the Distance 95

THE TRIANGULATION METHOD OF MEASURING THE PUTT

prepare to make my stroke, "This is a 42-foot putt I am going to sink right now." It is a method of providing a foundation for my confidence. The other reason for measuring is obvious. It simply makes good sense to know the distance of a given putt. When you know the length of the putt, you know the amount of power you need behind your putt.

I also like a method for measuring the length of a putt that I call "triangulation." This method works best on putts between 10 and 25 feet in length. I place myself at the apex of an equilateral triangle, the base being the line from the hole to my ball. Using my putter as an indicator, I visually divide the triangle in half, as illustrated on page 95, so that it becomes fairly easy to determine the approximate length of the base. Of course, the length of the base is the same as the length of my putt.

In using this method, I suggest that you place yourself on the "down" side of your "borrow" line. It seems to me to be easier to gauge the distance on a "borrowed" putt from the side opposite the "borrow." To explain more fully, let us imagine that we have a 20-foot putt on a green sloping down from right to left with a one-foot "borrow" to the right. The "down" side is to your left.

Another method I use regularly consists of imagining three concentric circles around the cup—a 15-foot circle, a 30-foot circle, and a 45-foot circle. This type of survey is obviously better for the longer putts. In the chapter on fundamentals, when we discussed how hard to hit a putt, you will remember that I broke the different types of putts into three categories, according to the strength of putt required: the hand putt, for putts 15 feet and shorter; the hand and forearm putt, for putts 15 to 30 feet in length; and the hand, arm, and shoulder putt, for putts 45 feet and over. By thinking in these terms and measuring the particularly long putts, I find that I am not constricted by the thought of a short backswing on a long putt, but rather am "freed" in my thinking and am thus more relaxed in the definite knowledge that I will need to use my hands, arms, and shoulders, as well as a longer backswing on a long putt. Remember that distance is measured in mathematical terms and can be coped with more easily by the application of mathematics.

Measuring the putt by the methods I have pointed out ties in with your regular practice routine, too. As I will point out, you should practice putting at "known" distances. Thus, when you are confronted with a 35-foot putt, for example, all you have to do is men-

Measuring the Distance 97

MEASURING THE DISTANCE OF THE PUTT

Here Dawson Taylor is measuring the distance of his putt by actually pacing it off. He does not walk all the way to the pin but merely estimates the last several yards so that his spikes will not disturb the turf around the cup. Note, too, that he does not walk on the "line" of his putt, but well to the side, for the same reason—so as not to ruffle the green.

tally remind yourself that this putt is just 5 feet shorter than all those 40-footers you were practicing the other day, and so you just need to hit it a little bit easier. This gives further foundation to the confidence of your stroke and the positive attitude that is so important to golf.

"Spot" Putting

Some fix upon a spot to play over before addressing the ball.
SIR W. G. SIMPSON, *The Art of Golf, 1887*

I AM A FIRM BELIEVER in the usefulness of "spot" putting. What is "spot" putting? Well, no doubt you have all seen the range-finders on a bowling lane—the diamond-like markers about one-third of the way down the maples. I know, as a matter of fact, that between 75 and 90 per cent of all the good bowlers in this country use these range-finders because they find it easier to hit a target 15 feet in front of them than one 60 feet away.

Obviously, it is easier to aim at and hit a target within a few feet of the ball than it is to aim at and hit a target two to ten times as far away. I am invariably able to find some small discoloration in the green, or an old divot mark, or a blade of clover, or some similar distinguishing mark either on or near my proposed putting line. When faced with a 10-foot putt, I like to find a "spot" about 3 feet in front of my ball; on 30-footers, I might find one 10 to 12 feet away; while on a very long putt, my "spot" might turn into a whole "area" or patch over which I will attempt to roll the ball.

Not only is my target closer when I putt at a spot, but in addition I am able to banish from my mind awareness of the entire line to the hole, particularly on a "borrowed" putt. For no matter how much I may have emphasized the point that we do not "aim" for the cup on borrowed putts, but rather aim along the *intended line,* we are all human and anxious to get the ball in the hole and are subject to a tendency to apply "body english," aim a little toward the hole, and forget the "box" principle.

Furthermore, I will assure you that if you develop the technique of spot putting you will be much less apt to raise your head after you have stroked the ball, simply because you don't have to look as far to see whether your ball is moving in the right direction.

On very short putts, especially sharp-breaking putts, find your spot to the right or left of the cup, depending upon the direction of the break. Then aim for your spot, avoiding any tendency to aim for the cup. You will miss considerably fewer short putts if you do.

There is something psychologically sound about spot putting. It gives you the added confidence that is so helpful on the putting green.

A Discussion of "Grain"

Ladies Professional Golf Association Record

Fewest Putts: *21, by Judy Kimball in 1961 American Women's Open, Minneapolis, Minnesota*

MY EARLY PUTTING experience gave me a quick and unforgettable knowledge of the effect of "grain" on the track of the ball during a putt. In my home we had a long, narrow hallway with a velour type of carpet laid down its entire length. By the hour, I used to putt from one end of the hallway to the other, into one of those metal, dishlike cups that has a tilted entrance to capture the ball when it rolls up and onto it.

Although I was certain that I was stroking the ball in a perfectly straight line, every time the ball neared the "cup" it seemed to veer radically to the left and "hook" into the cup. At no time was I able to putt without getting this strange result. I tried reversing the "putting green" and putted toward the west. Lo, the opposite occurred; the ball would "slice" into the cup. I came to the conclusion that some factor in the method of manufacture of the carpet was causing this unusual result and decided that it was related to the way the nap of the carpet lay. When the ball rolled from west to east, the nap of the carpet leaned toward my left and carried the ball to the left with it, especially as it slowed down in the latter part of its track.

By the same token, it became evident to me that the reverse was occurring when I putted toward the west—the nap was reversed and the ball turned right at the end of its trip.

Probably because I practiced regularly from the west end of that upstairs hallway, to this day I prefer to stroke right-to-left-breaking putts, whether the break is caused by an actual rise in the ground to the right of the cup or by the grain in the grass "leaning" from right to left. "Grain," as you have probably gathered by now, is nothing more than an indication of the direction the grass grows on the putting green. You can illustrate this for yourself by moving the blade of

A Discussion of "Grain"

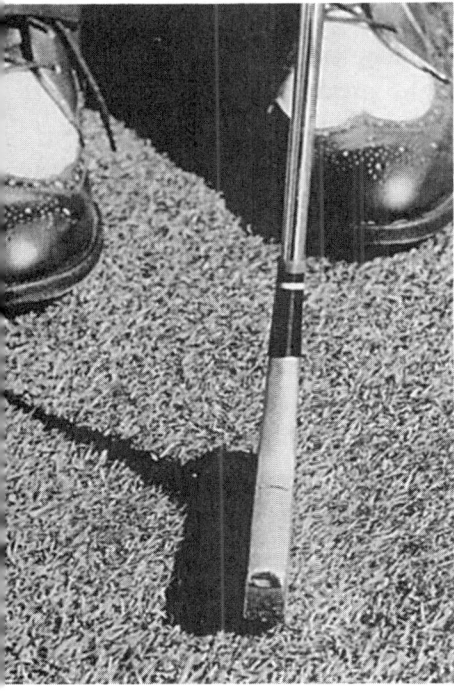

"With the Grain" and "Against the Grain"

Though you may find it hard to believe, these two "rubs of the putting green" by my putter were made at precisely the same spot. Notice the "forest" raised in the photograph at the right. Always remember that putting with the grain speeds the ball, and putting against the grain slows it up.

your putter lightly one way and then the other in a flat position against the grass of your putting green. By doing this, you will "raise" the nap of the green.

If you raise a nap, as you can see being done in the photograph on page 101, you may be sure that the green is "grainy" and that you will probably have to allow for its effect on your putting line.

Greens seeded with a Bermuda grass have a particularly strong "grain." Golfers in the South, where Bermuda grass predominates, have to be especially aware of its effect.

There are several methods of detecting grain, and I would suggest that you use them all. Of course, under the rules of golf it is forbidden to "raise the nap" of the green as I have indicated in the photographs. Under Rule 35-1-F, you learn that "a player shall not test the surface of the putting green by rolling a ball or roughening or scraping the surface." So look carefully at the way the grass is growing, especially around and near the cup. You can quite often see the way the blades of grass are "leaning" in one direction or another.

Another method for determining whether the grass is "grainy," as well as whether it is fast, is to look for a "shine" off the green. This "shine" is the reflection of the sun on the grass. When you see the green "shine" you can be certain that it is on the "fast" side and you can also be fairly certain that the green is "grainy." Usually you can tell from the shine which way the grain runs, since the shine occurs when the grass is bent over on its side and a fuller surface of the individual blade is exposed to the sun. Thus, where the shine is most prominent you can figure the grain is running away from you.

Be alert, too, for the way water would run off a green. Where the water flows down from a mound or plateau you can be certain that it has caused the grass to bend in the direction it flows.

Now, what do you do about putting with and against the grain? The answer is simple and yet, as I have pointed out in our earlier discussion of "tolerance for error," sometimes we must let our intelligence disregard everything our instinct tells us. I'll never know why it is so difficult for me (and, I'm certain, for many other golfers as well), when I know that the grain is directly against me and that it will slow up the putt, to hit the putt hard enough against the grain to be "up" to the cup. One trick I have used, and you may try it too, is to imagine a tee about 6 inches beyond the cup and to putt for the imaginary tee. Sometimes it works. I have left many a putt hanging

A Discussion of "Grain"

on the front lip of the cup as a result of my failure to recognize the strength of the grain in a green.

The reverse situation, putting with the grain, is not as hard for the ordinary golfer to adapt to. The ball will travel faster and farther than you expect, so grip your putter a little more lightly than usual and pretend you are putting downhill. You might try the reverse "psychology" of imagining a tee or the cup several inches closer than it actually is.

Putting successfully "across the grain," whether right to left or left to right, is primarily a matter of long experience. You will have to experiment on putts of various lengths. I have seen, on occasion, an absolutely level 6-foot putt carried 2 inches off-line as a result of failure to realize the effect of grain.

I also remember well playing at the Homestead course in Hot Springs, Virginia, and having an elderly caddie indicate to me on a 20-foot putt that I should putt 3 feet to the right of the cup, when I could see that the putt ought to break from left to right. I scoffed at him, and to show him that he was "crazy," I putted where he had indicated the line. Behold! Down went the putt! The Homestead course is a famous one and is built in the mountains. Let me warn you that mountain courses are notoriously grainy. When your elderly caddie tells you where to putt, I would suggest that you take his advice!

Putting on so-called quartering grain—neither with the grain nor against it—is also a matter of experience which you will have to gain, in many cases, "after the deed has been accomplished"—after you have missed the putt and are trying to determine why in a "post mortem" examination of the green.

In general, remember that the grain of a green affects the track of the ball most when the ball is slowing down in the last stages of its trip. So in order to neutralize the effect of grain, especially on your shorter holing-out efforts, putt boldly and with a firm stroke when you encounter grain, and you will be more successful in the long run. And always take the advice of that elderly caddie!

Psychology of Putting

Every time the ball left his [Smith's] putter it was almost sure to drop and in that brilliant spell he holed out from all distances from two to ten yards. The only putt he missed was a "small one" of about four yards on the 14th green.
                    NEWS ITEM: GLASGOW, SCOTLAND. JUNE 1933.

I PUTT BEST when "my hands feel thin." This is an old expression attributed to Douglas Edgar, and is the only one which, to my mind, clearly expresses the feeling I have in advance of a good round of putting. I never *know* whether I am going to hole a great many putts, because there are too many outside factors involved for me to be certain of that. All I know is that I seem to have a sensitivity in my fingertips that makes the putter feel like a magic wand over which I have complete control.

There is a great deal to be said for adequate physical and mental preparation in any sport, but it is particularly vital in as "temperamental" a sport as golf. Sometimes I wonder what might have happened to the evolution of the game if back in the early days of golf those avid Scotsmen had not insisted upon absolute silence when they swung their "shinney sticks." Perhaps if the roars of the crowd on the baseball diamond or the gridiron were allowed today on the tournament trail of golf the cases of "nerves" might not be so pronounced.

The anticipation that "I will play well today" starts with a leisurely arising in the morning and a comfortably slow and easy dressing for the day. Just as I try to prepare myself for a "paced" or unhurried approach to my game, so should you do the same.

How often I see the busy Saturday-afternoon throng of businessmen rush into the parking lots with their cars, toss their clubs to a caddie, and hurry up the stairs to the locker room with perhaps a yell toward the first tee, "Tell Joe I'll be right down and to wait for me."

I try to avoid anything which will upset my equilibrium before the game. If I think my mail might bring bad news, I postpone opening it until later. The amateur golfer should be as careful to get the maximum enjoyment from a game of golf as the most hardened professional golfer. If you are going to play golf at 1:00 P.M. on a busy Saturday, you should realize that you will have to allow a certain amount of time to get to the course, to dress, to practice a little, perhaps to eat a light lunch, and to be ready to play a comfortable game. Even if you are a "once-a-weeker," with some intelligent planning you can increase your enjoyment of your golf game. One of the best ways of increasing your enjoyment is to cut down the number of your strokes. And one of the best ways to accomplish this is to allow enough time for some leisurely practice on the putting green before you begin to play.

Quite often the practice green which is available before your "big round" is of a different type of grass, often even cut at a different height than the greens you will encounter out on the course. So, instead of plunking down a ball on the putting green and immediately making a try for a hole 25 feet away, be smart! Realize that the most important thing you can do is to start building up your confidence in your putting ability in general and putting stroke in particular. So start about 18 inches away from the hole in the most level putting area you can find and take four balls and put them down around that cup in a circle. Knock each one of them in with the firmest stroke you can muster. Your confidence will start to grow immediately. Pay particular attention to keeping your grip relaxed and to hitting the ball below center so as to give it the end-over-end roll which is so desirable. You might even take just one ball and, after placing it with the name on its "equator," check to see whether or not it is rolling without a wobble.

After you have holed a number of straight, level, short putts, I suggest that you try to find a practice hole with a left-to-right slope. Then, of course, after you have knocked a few left-to-right putts into the hole, putt from the opposite side of the cup in a position which will require the same amount of "borrow," and knock in a few right-to-left putts. Don't be surprised or upset at missing a few of these. You will at first. The important thing is to end your practice with a holed putt—perhaps even two or three in a row. Don't ever end your practice on a missed putt, even if you find it necessary to get closer to the hole.

You should only practice longer putts, however, after you have holed a number of short putts. When you do, work from known distances, so that you can be registering in your mind the strength it is taking to hit the distance you see. Watch to see that your backswing is free and easy, that your hands and arm muscles are relaxed, and that the blade of your putter stays "square."

It is entirely possible that in the past you have never carried out such an intensive, yet intelligent, practice putting session before a round of golf. I would like to assure you that if you will try such a method of practicing, your enjoyment and appreciation of the game of golf, not to mention the "game within the game," putting will be enhanced immeasurably. Such a practice procedure need not last more than ten minutes in order to pay off in a grooved stroke that may save you from one to five strokes on your round. And the confidence that you gain from knowing that even if you "spray" a few shots you can probably recover and sink a putt or two will help your long game. You will not need to try so hard to "thread the needle" to the pin and be so close you can't afford to miss. Even the 10-footers for pars, while never actually enjoyable, are much less fearsome when your putting stroke is sound and you know it.

A moment ago I spoke about my never knowing whether I'm going to hole a great many putts in an upcoming round even when I know I'm putting well. At this point, with respect to the psychology of putting, I should like to call your attention to the odds on holing a particular putt. I see so many golfers, especially high handicappers, get violently upset at missing, say, a 10-foot putt or even a 3-foot putt. Now I must admit that there is greater reason to become angry at missing the shorter putt, but I feel that very few golfers, even low handicappers, have ever carefully considered the odds on making putts of various lengths.

In practice sessions of my own, I have holed as many as twenty to twenty-five 10-foot or 12-foot putts in a row and immediately followed them with four or five straight clean misses at the same distance and from exactly the same spot. However, I try not to let these misses disturb me. By practicing from a constant distance, 10 feet for example, on a practice green, I get to know about how many out of ten I should hole. Perhaps one day I'll hole twelve out of twenty, on another day ten out of twenty, and on another eight. Some days, I can even run it up to an average of fifteen.

Then I switch to a 20-foot distance and try the same thing in order to see how many out of ten I can hole. I use no more than four or

Psychology of Putting

five balls because one will often block the path to the cup and interfere with the next putt. Of course, I get a great deal of exercise, good for the waistline, leaning over to pick the balls out of the cup. Again, in my mind, my "computer" is figuring the averages as well as noting the distance and taking into account the smoothness of my stroke, while it is saying "you can make about five or six, or even seven out of twenty 20-footers, can't you?"

Thus, when I am out on the course and am faced with a 20-footer on my very first green, the first thought that crosses my mind is that my chances of making this putt are about 1 in 3 to 1 in 4. So when I don't hole it (I hope I came close!), I say to myself, "Well, don't be upset at missing that one. You stroked it well, but the odds that you would make it were low anyway."

Remember, too, that the various imperfections in the green itself, sometimes completely undetectable in advance, tend to decrease the odds of your making a particular putt. On the practice green you have been putting on the smoothest possible track you could find. The regular green might be spike-marked from the all-day tramping of not-too-gentle golf shoes. This is why the early starters on the golf course very often have a great advantage over the late starters and why, quite often, a good score posted early in the last day of a big tournament will withstand all attempts to match it. Late in the day, when the greens have hardened from the heat of the sun and have been scuffed up by many spikes, your chances of holing your usual quota have decreased.

Many times I have found myself, during late rounds, approaching greens that are hard, bumpy, and pocked with divots and spike marks, with a mental attitude acquired from putting on fresh greens that "track right." Then, if I miss the kind of putt I have been making previously, I get discouraged. A subtle change in attitude occurs, and instead of knowing I'll make the putt, I start hoping I won't miss it. This change in attitude is both common and foolish. One has to adjust one's expectations to the conditions and be aware of the odds.

It might be interesting to tell you my own experience in winning the •Masters Tournament in 1934. Craig Wood had gotten an early start, had posted a score of 285, and then had left for the East without waiting to see whether he would win or not. So, early in my round, when I was on the fourth hole, I knew that I needed a par 72 to win by 1 stroke, that is, provided no one else managed to come up with a sensational last round to better Wood's score. At the seventeenth tee I needed one birdie in the last two holes. Fortunately, my third shot on the seventeenth was a short pitch. I hit it to within 12 feet of the hole on a beautifully level spot on the green and quite confidently stroked the ball in for the birdie I so badly needed.

The Augusta National course at that time was played with its present nines reversed, so the eighteenth hole that I needed only to play in par was the present ninth hole, a short 4-par. The hole wasn't presenting too much difficulty, but the wind was blowing hard and the greens were very hard, almost "swept out" by the wind. There was a trap guarding the short left side of the hole, and in trying to play it safe for my 4, I got well over the trap and found my ball about 35 feet above and beyond the cup, with a slick downhill left-to-right putt coming up. Although I knew very well that I should get "up" to the cup so as to leave myself a short right-to-left second putt —a much easier one to hole under the circumstances—I felt that I could borrow quite a bit from the left hill and "drift" the ball down close for an easy second putt. I was both surprised and disappointed in myself when I borrowed too much. The ball stopped above the cup from 3 to 3½ feet away, leaving me a fast downhill putt with a quick left-to-right break—dreaded by even the most skillful putter.

I studied the putt, and at that moment I had one of those "positive" thoughts: Since the green was slippery and the break was fast, all I could do was hit the ball firmly and squarely. I was also aware that even if I didn't hole the putt, I could tie for the title and have at least an even chance to win in a play-off. So I stepped up and knocked the ball right in, to win.

Afterwards, a number of people came up to me and said, "You certainly were confident of that last putt on eighteen, weren't you?" Although I didn't admit it then, I'll say now that it was one of the "longest" putts I ever holed, and I am certain that it was due to my attitude and nothing else. It was the positive thought that paid off.

Technical Problems and Their Solutions

Diegel and I met in the quarter-finals. I had trailed all day. However, I was never willing to concede until the last shot was played and with 2 down and 2 to play, I made a last-stretch sprint. The seventeenth at Olympia Fields is a two-shot hole with a ditch in front of the green. Leo's second went into the ditch. I played a shot, hole-high, to the left of the flag some fifteen feet away. Leo got out nicely, just on the green, leaving him a forty-foot putt.

I was not paying too much attention for I figured the best he could get was a 5. I was left with a putt I'd be unable to stop near the hole, for the contour of the green was such that it started from nothing and bulged hog-back below my line of putt. Then it slanted upward sharply at the back edge. Mentally considering all these facts I was suddenly aware that Leo had holed his long putt for a par 4. I had to hole out for a 3. . . . It was one of the most difficult putts I ever faced, for my ball would gain momentum going down this incline of some ten feet or more. I was 2 down. I was on the green in two. I had to sink that putt to win the hole and I had to win the hole to stay in the running.

I elected to putt away from the hole. I noticed a small leaf at the top of the green and I used it for a target. First, I had to stop the forward and upward progress of my ball at just the right point so that, when stopped, the ball would pick up its own momentum and trickle down the slope to the hole. Second, I had to hit dead center because if I hit at either edge of the hole, the ball would not stay in the cup, with the momentum it was bound to pick up. I took my stance and stroked the ball upward toward my target leaf. . . . It reached the leaf, hesitated momentarily, then angled obliquely to roll down the slope and drop dead into the cup. Winning the seventeenth by means of such a crucial and extremely difficult putt assured me of the win of the eighteenth, for the shock of the putt was entirely too much for Leo.

WALTER HAGEN

PUTTING THE LEVEL PUTT

Obviously, this is the most simple and uncomplicated situation you will encounter on the putting green. So let's review a few fundamentals and concentrate on a smooth, low, "level-to-the-turf" stroke, for you can forget any problems that would result from a slope in the green.

Remember the "box" principle. Your left elbow is "aiming" along the "right-angle" line parallel to your true putting line in the level putt. Your feet are in "square" position—at right angles to the putting line. Your head is immobile, your knees slightly bent in the "sitting-down" position. Your left-hand grip is firm, your right-hand grip is delicate. You have taken a deep breath and relaxed, and you are ready to putt. Don't forget to hit through the ball with the right hand against a firm left hand and wrist!

PUTTING AN UPHILL PUTT

The emphasis in this situation is on firmness—even boldness. So often one sees the inexperienced and occasionally even the top-flight golfers short on their uphill putts. I recommend putting for an imaginary cup 3 to 6 inches beyond the actual cup so that mentally you will give yourself the courage to reach the cup. The uphill putt that reaches the cup often "holes out," since there is little tendency on the part of the golfer to be so bold as to overrun the cup seriously. Remember "Uphill: Firmness and boldness," and you will hole many an uphill putt. Suggestion: Remove the pin or have it tended.

Putting the Downhill Putt

Whenever you are putting downhill, the emphasis should be on lightness of touch and delicacy of judgment. Especially when the green is on the "fast" side it is particularly important that you try to stop your putt close to the cup, preferably slightly past the cup, should you not hole out in your first stroke, inasmuch as the return uphill putt will be easier than another delicate, short, downhill putt. Grasp your putter very lightly with the fingertips of your right hand, still keeping your left hand firm. Sometimes it helps to hit the ball away from the "sweet spot" and out toward the toe of your putter, in order to lessen the weight and momentum factor. These are difficult putts and often it is best not to be too bold for fear of overrunning the cup and missing on the way back. Suggestion: Leave the pin in on downhill putts unless you can see that it is in a position where it might keep your ball out of the hole.

Technical Problems and Their Solutions

PUTTING A SIDEHILL PUTT—LEFT TO RIGHT

On this type of putt, and also in the reverse situation which is discussed next, I believe it is wisest to disregard the actual cup and putt for an imaginary one instead. This instruction follows the old golfer's adage: "All putts are straight, the cup just isn't where it is supposed to be." Shifting your aim to an imaginary cup also enables you to adhere to the "box" principle.

On a sidehill putt where you must borrow from the left and break to the right, simply imagine a cup to the left of the actual cup. The distance to the left from the real cup to the imaginary cup should be determined by the amount of roll you figure on after the ball breaks. Once you have established the position of the imaginary cup and the line to it, orient your stance to the new line exactly as you would to a level cup. Try to block out any inclination to aim for the real cup in order to avoid "lunging" toward it with your arms.

Remember the "margin of error" and allow for it either by moving the imaginary cup slightly more to the left or by closing the blade of your putter a little. The important thing is to approach the cup from the "high" side, for if you do you will be turning to your advantage the tendency of the ball to roll downhill.

PUTTING A SIDEHILL PUTT—RIGHT TO LEFT

Most right-handed golfers find it easier to putt the right-to-left-breaking putt than the reverse putt, the left-to-right. There are several good reasons for this, but primarily it is because while taking up his stance in the right-to-left-break situation the golfer must rotate his body clockwise. He would then be hitting "into his line," which is to say that he is moving his putter blade back from the ball on a line "inside" his normal line. This happens because the turf is higher out toward the toe of the club and thus almost forces the blade "inside" during the backswing. It is somewhat easier for the golfer to swing from inside his normal line than from outside. The reverse is true in the left-to-right break because the putter blade is often forced outside the line as a result of the height of the turf under the heel of the putter blade.

So, being aware of these factors, it is wise to overcompensate to the right on the right-to-left putt either by placing your imaginary cup and the imaginary line to it slightly farther to the right or else by laying your club face open a bit, in a slight clockwise turn.

It is also obvious that since your imaginary cup is to the right of the true cup, your stance and your stroke will be oriented to the imaginary line, not to the actual line to the cup. You must have the "courage of your convictions"—the confidence in your ability—to estimate the amount of roll, and then act upon your decision with a firm, low, level-to-the-turf stroke. And don't forget to come in on the "high" side of the cup, which in this case is the right side.

Technical Problems and Their Solutions 115

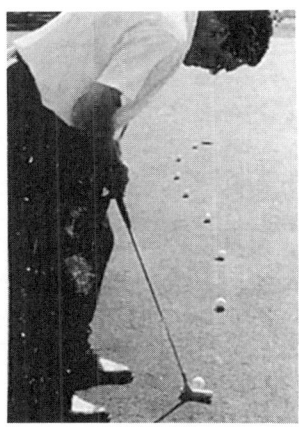

PUTTING THE DOUBLE ROLL

You will have to look closely at the two pictures above in order to discern the difference between them. They are both representations of a double roll in the green—that is, one which will alternately carry the ball left and then right. For simplicity's sake, let us assume that this putt is exactly 20 feet long. Our study of the first 10 feet of the putt tells us that the ball will break 6 inches to the left. Next, our study of the last 10 feet of the putt convinces us that the ball will break exactly the same distance, 6 inches, to the right as it nears the cup.

Now, simple logic would suggest that you should aim 6 inches to the right of the cup. Theoretically the ball would then break 6 inches to the left during the first 10 feet of its path; it would at this point be heading to the left of the cup; and it would then break 6 inches to the right and end up in the cup. This is what is portrayed in the left-hand picture.

Actually, the right-hand picture is a more accurate illustration of what happens in this situation. While in the left-hand picture the two "bends" of the proposed track of the ball are of equal curvature, in the right-hand picture the first part of the track is much straighter and the second part of the track more curved. This is explained by the fact that during the first part of the putt the ball is still being affected more by the power of the club than by the contour of the hill, while during the latter part of the putt the slope of the green will have a greater effect on the roll of the ball.

So when you undertake a putt which is going to have a "double roll," you should not aim as far to the right or left of the cup as you would normally be inclined to do. There is really no formula for successful double-roll putting. Experience will teach you how best to cope with the situation. But once you learn to recognize the "double roll" and apply the correct principles, you will find that you can perform wizardry with your putter.

PUTTING TO A PLATEAU PIN POSITION

Note the tilt of the pin in the hole. You should leave this pin in the hole, as there will be a lot of room for your ball to get in the front of the hole.

Specialty Shots with the Putter

Within narrow limits there is a choice of styles of good putting. It may be done entirely from the wrist, from the shoulder, or by a combined use of all the arm joints.
SIR W. G. SIMPSON, *The Art of Golf, 1887*

SINCE THE PUTTER has little or no loft, it is an ideal club at times when you want to keep the ball close to the ground. Very few golfers are aware of the utility of the putter in such situations as illustrated below.

On the tenth hole of the south course at the Detroit Golf Club there is a nasty but shallow trap on the right-hand side of the green. The green itself is a bit elevated. Also to the right and close to the tenth green is a large overspreading oak tree. A pushed tee shot which ends up under this oak tree usually spells trouble for the average golfer, particularly since the trap lies between the tree and the green. He usually thinks he has to use an iron with the right loft to avoid the branches and still get him over the trap. This usually ends up being an iron with too little loft to supply the backspin necessary to stop the ball on the green, and to add to his woes, there is still another trap beyond the green. Alas, too often he reconciles himself to hitting the branches and playing his next shot from the near trap, or getting under the branches, over-running the green, and then playing his next shot back to the pin from the far trap.

The golfer who is aware of his putter solves this problem much more easily, for, fortunately, the ground is usually baked quite hard underfoot and is also fairly level. Furthermore, the sand in the trap is hard-packed and there is no appreciable "lip" on the trap. Several times in championship play I have seen our better players use the putter very successfully from this position. The ball is struck smartly off the left toe with a definite follow-through for overspin. It scoots first through the dry grass and then into the trap, where its overspin carries it up the front slope of the trap and pops it onto the green. At this point, its spin has usually diminished to the point where it will die. The result is often satisfactory and occasionally sensational. And, after all, even if the shot fails to come off (and it sometimes fails because of the timidity of the golfer and his failure to hit hard enough), the ball will probably end up in the trap, where it would have been anyway had the player used a 7 or 8 iron.

Not only should you watch for this type of "save" shot with a putter but you should also be wise enough to recognize the difficulty of a pitch shot near the edge of a green when the ball is lying on "concrete"—a very thin lie on hard ground—or even down in a pockmark such as that caused by a badly replaced divot. Sometimes it is necessary to "take your penalty" for an erring shot over a green. Many times a lie is so difficult or the odds are so great against a successfully lofted shot that it is senseless to try any club but the putter. And if you will practice a few of these trouble shots—"percentage shots" the pros call them—you will eventually be able to call yourself a "golfer."

Horton Smith confronts one of the major detriments to putting through a sand trap successfully. Here he is faced with a horrendous lie, where the ball has been caught beneath the large overhanging lip of a sand trap.

Specialty Shots with the Putter

Another position in which you should usually use your putter is on the fringe a few feet from the green. Granted that the fringe itself will slow up the ball; still the percentage is that you will get the ball somewhere near enough to the hole to make a 1-putt. Practice putting the ball from varying distances off the fringe of the practice green. If the ball is "sitting up" on top of the grass, be careful not to get too far under it, for fear of popping it up in the air and over the fringe. The fringe will then fail to slow the ball down to the extent that you had planned. Play this shot from your usual putting stance and be sure to follow through low and straight in order to get an overspinning ball.

My experience has proved that I usually do not have to hit such an approach putt nearly as hard as I would be inclined to do. For the overspin in such a putt from the fringe proves to be even more pronounced than in the normal putting stroke. So be careful in estimating the distance. If you tend to underestimate the power of your stroke, I believe you will be more successful.

When you putt your ball out of a "down lie"—that is, when the ball is down in deep grass—or in a "cuppy" lie with a tuft of grass behind it, your putting stroke should be more of a chop than the usual smooth stroke. Don't be afraid to try the "chop" technique with your putter when you are forced to, or when you feel the odds favor its success more than a shot with a lofted club. On the backswing, bring your blade up at a sharper angle than usual so that you can actually hit down on the ball. But be sure to follow through with a distinct "square blade." You will be most pleased at the way the ball will pop out of its troublesome lie and go merrily spinning on its way to the hole. There is one particular advantage to using your putter in such a situation: you are more apt to stay on line toward the pin. Then, if your gauge of distance happens to be good as well, you will have a most satisfactory result.

I have actually seen the 210-yard ninth hole at Oakland Hills driven with a putter against a strong wind! Granted that this was a freak shot—and a marvelous one—it still gives you an indication of what you can do against a strong wind with your putter. Your putter can also be used against a strong wind when you are uncertain of your ability to make a pitch shot "sit down" on a green. Of course, I would prefer that you try such shots to open greens rather than closely trapped ones.

I had an excellent example of such a use of my putter when I won

PUTTING FROM THE FRINGE

Specialty Shots with the Putter 121

the St. Paul Open one year. I knew I could afford to go 1 over par on the last hole, a moderate 4-par, so I had hit my second shot to a spot some 20 yards in front of the green. The pin was about one-third of the way back from the front of the green at the top of a rise. A most ghastly thought occurred to me when I realized that if I pitched to the pin too strongly, I would go over the rise and very possibly 3-putt coming back to the hole from the back of the green.

It was fall and the ground was hard. I decided to putt the ball and be very careful not to go over the rise. I tried to be about 10 feet short, but in my anxiety I hit the putt a bit too hard and the ball rolled up, not 10 feet short, but only 2 feet short.

I dropped the putt and won the tournament but I'll never forget the nightmare I had later on about pitching over that pin!

PUTTING TO A PLATEAU OR OVER A CREST

The problems of putting to a plateau and over a crest are undoubtedly among the most difficult in golf. Their satisfactory solution can result in great stroke saving. The most important thing to realize when putting to a cup on a plateau or over a crest is that it is necessary at all costs to be "up" to the cup with your putt, or at least over the crest or edge of the plateau. Being short of the crest or not up onto the plateau can be disastrous, inasmuch as the ball is very likely to roll back down the slope and even if it doesn't your next putt will be very difficult to judge and execute successfully.

Quite often you will find that this type of putt is best executed as an "area" or "spot" putt, in which you attempt to stop the ball at a spot or area just over the crest or edge of the plateau and allow the slight momentum of the ball to carry it from there to the cup.

Look over your line very carefully. Since you will be attempting to make the ball "die at the cup," you must overestimate the degree of roll to the left or right, because the slow-moving "dying putt" will be "taking the roll" more than a putt that is still moving fast.

Don't necessarily try to hole this kind of putt. Sometimes it is better to "lag it up" close and hope to hole the next one than to bang away and still end up two putts away. Be extra firm in your grip, because you will be putting uphill. Leave the pin in; it may help to stop the ball and even help to hole it. Settle for a 2-putt any time and be glad of it!

USING THE PUTTER AS A "TEXAS WEDGE" FROM OFF THE GREEN

The ball should be struck smartly in forward position with definite overspin imparted. If the ball is "down" into the grass, the stroke approximates a "chop" but the follow-through is distinct and low, to give the ball "run." This shot is especially useful on a close lie where the terrain to the cup is fairly level.

Specialty Shots with the Putter

Putting Out of a Trap

The shot illustrated above is one of the "trick shots" of golf. I believe that Walter Hagen was one of the first of the great golfers who became famous for his ability to putt out of traps.

There are certain conditions which must exist before this shot is practicable. First, the ball must be sitting up very cleanly on dry sand. If it is the least bit "down" into the sand, the shot can be muffed very easily. Second, the surface of the trap itself should be at least smooth if not hard, because soft, feathery sand tends to muffle the strength of the blow and may prevent you from getting out of the trap at all. Third, the trap should be shallow, as it is difficult to make the ball run up the face of a deep trap without losing much if not all of its speed and spin. Fourth, the trap should be clean-cut at its upper "lip"—that is, it should have no overhang which might catch the ball and prevent it from getting out. Finally, the pin position should be some distance away from the edge of the trap, because with the overspin which is imparted to the ball, this type of shot is impossible to stop quickly once it is out of the trap, and must have some room to roll. This last consideration is not an absolute prerequisite, because the average golfer might wish to sacrifice nearness to the pin for safety and might be satisfied with being out of the trap and anywhere on the green.

Now, as for the mechanics of putting out of a trap: They are very much the same as for any long putt. The overspin imparted to the ball will cause it to roll across the top of the sand in the bunker, climb the face of the trap, and spin out forward onto the green. You should apply a bit of shoulder action and the ball should be played carefully forward—off the left foot—so as to be certain to impart the overspin. There should be a distinct and low follow-through which, if anything, should be exaggerated, so that you will not loft the ball into the side of the trap and risk burying it.

Remember that you are in a hazard and that you dare not sole your putter blade any more than you would your sand-wedge. Practice this shot a great deal before you try it in a match. It is tricky, but a very satisfying result can often be obtained from it.

The Short-Putt "Jab" Technique

There is nothing—I speak from experience—in a round of either match or medal competition that bears down with quite the pressure of having continually to hole out putts of three and four feet; the kind left by overly enthusiastic approaches.

ROBERT T. JONES, JR.

DURING THE LAST several years, the pro circuit has introduced the expression "jab" technique as a description of a new method of holing short putts at a distance around 3 feet from the cup. In discussing this technique, I should like to point out the excellent skill with which Billy Casper holes these somewhat dangerous putts. He hits through the ball with a positive right-hand motion, against what you might term "resistance" on the part of the left hand. In other words, it is almost as if his left hand were saying, "Nothing is going to let this club head twist or turn when it hits the ball. I don't care whether it goes through the ball or not, but when that right hand comes in there to hit the ball, I am going to be set so securely that the right hand and the action that it produces are not going to twist the club out of line." This technique is, in actuality, a "braking" action on the part of the left hand. The result is that there is practically no follow-through. Casper has extreme control of the muscles of his left hand and arm, and the result is a steadier stroke, and a more dependable one under pressure conditions.

I don't think this stroke should really be called a "jab." This term implies a lack of control, which is not the case. It is actually a way of gaining added control on short putts. It distributes the work load evenly between the two hands. In a "jab" putt, the right hand supplies the motive power, while the left hand controls the position of the blade.

Now, to review short-putt "jab" technique. Remember that the stroke is shorter, sharper, and firmer, with less emphasis on the follow-through. It is more mechanical. Remember that as the ball loses its momentum it is more apt to be thrown off by the imperfections in the turf around the cup—the spike marks of other golfers and variations in the grass. So the more you are able to neutralize these outside effects on your short putt, the more effectively you will hole the ball. With the "jab" technique, it is easier to putt for the center of the cup. This also provides a psychological lift, because you no longer have to worry about so many outside factors affecting the result of your putt.

Practice

Today I know of many golfers who are only second- or third-rate golfers, but whose skill as putters is all that keeps them in the rank that they do hold. . . . My personal opinion is that more men are good putters from practice than because they have any pronounced superiority, to begin with, over other men.

FRANCIS OUIMET

NO ONE CAN ACHIEVE any degree of success in any sport without practice. This goes both for those of us who have great natural ability and those who have only average ability. Practice in putting is particularly valuable because it can help the individual with only average athletic ability to become an outstanding golfer.

One basic problem is that of motivation. You have that problem half solved already because if you didn't *want* to improve your putting you wouldn't be reading this book. Another problem for most of us is lack of time; the everyday demands of living simply don't allow us to spend that much time at the golf course. However, you don't necessarily have to be on the practice green in order to practice your putting. For one thing, you can spend a little time every day "thinking" putting wherever you may happen to be. You can go even further than merely thinking and pick up the letter opener on your desk or the paring knife by the kitchen sink and work on hooding the left hand and wrist, for example.

Besides practicing mentally, you can also practice putting in your home, but we'll get to that later. Right now, let's consider the proper methods of working on the practice-putting green.

Practice

HOW TO PRACTICE ON THE PRACTICE-PUTTING GREEN

A good starting routine is to putt a few balls, one after the other, into the cup from a foot to a foot and a half away from the cup. Concentrate on the smoothness of your stroke and on hitting the center of the cup.

Next, putt five or six balls from approximately the same location, first from a level spot, then from one which will cause the ball to break from right to left, and finally from one which will break from left to right. Be sure to measure your distance each time so that you can register in your mind the necessary power needed at each given distance. Gradually lengthen your distance from the cup.

Narrowing the Cup

Next, start to narrow the approach to the cup by placing a golf ball on one side or the other, so that you have less room to enter the cup. You may also do this by placing bright-colored tees on either side of the cup. Practice making the ball "die" first on the front edge of the cup and then on the "top" side of the cup. Charge yourself a fine each time you fail to get "up" to the cup.

Practice 129

PUTTING TO A TEE

This is probably the finest possible practice for developing your "touch" for distance. It also serves to make the regular cup seem like a wash tub by comparison, when you get out onto the course. Always measure your practice distance, even if only by pacing it off. Try placing two tees 10 feet apart on a sloped green, and practice from one to the other. This will help you on "breaking" putts in both directions. Gradually increase your distance, always measuring it and making a mental note of the distance.

PRACTICE FOR DEVELOPING A "DISCRIMINATING TOUCH"

By placing two tees 6 inches apart and then putting first to one and then the other you will develop your touch so that you can make the ball "die" at the hole more often. Try this exercise, first at close distances and then gradually at greater distances, until you can control the ball at lengths of 15, 20, or even 25 feet.

MORE PRACTICE TECHNIQUES

This photograph illustrates the practice of holing the ball first on one side of the cup, then at the center, and then on the other side of the cup. It is a wonderful way to demonstrate to yourself that you *must* enter the high side of the cup on a "borrow" putt. It is also a useful adjunct to your practice with the colored tees, because you are further pinpointing your target.

"Putting up the Shadow"

Usually you can find a level spot on the green which will enable you to take advantage of the shadow of the pin to help you visualize your line to the hole. This practice is particularly useful in giving you a mental picture of your "square-bladed" follow-through along the shadow line.

A Further Refinement of "Putting up the Shadow"

After you have practiced awhile along the relatively short length of the shadow, practice longer putts at 20-foot, 25-foot, and 30-foot distances. Always keep a score of your successes and failures. If you figure out how many you can sink out of ten tries, you will be better able to figure your odds on sinking putts of varying lengths.

HOW TO PRACTICE AT HOME

How can I encourage you to practice your stroke at home? Well, I will tell you that practice during the off-season will pay off a hundred times over in the achievement of better results in the spring, and it will provide you with self-satisfaction at the accomplishment of a very worthwhile end.

Even I will admit that until the recent invention of ball-return mechanisms, it was not much fun to practice putting on the carpet at home. But now the irritation of chasing the errant golf ball under the easy chair has been ended. Even when you miss your practice putt at home, your ball will come rolling merrily back to you, thanks to the return mechanism, a product of the modern inventive mind.

There are also types of carpet that can be put down over your own floor and that simulate very well the usual surface of a golf green. So, with some of the drawbacks eliminated, it can even be fun to practice putting away from the golf course. Another important factor is that with very few outside distractions (unless the television is on!), you are able, for the time being, to forget about whether you are sinking your putts or whether you are up to or short of the cup, and can concentrate on the most important phase of your putting game—your stroke. That is to say, you can focus on your stroking technique to an extent completely impossible on the regular practice green. With some of my suggestions and the photographs here, you may be stimulated to try improving your putting at home. So let me recommend to you certain putting practice procedures which you may find useful. Even if you do not attempt all of these methods, the adoption of any one of them will help to strengthen your putting ability.

First and foremost, work on the "square-blade" principle—the low stroke with hooded left wrist and arched right wrist. Get a ruler or a yardstick, or a 2 by 2 or two parallel 2 by 2's about 18 inches long, and practice taking your blade away from a "square-to-the-line" position and keeping it square as long as possible, as well as low, and close to the carpet.

Practice putting with the right hand alone as shown in the illustration on page 58. Also try pushing the ball with the right hand only, so as to develop a sense of alignment and the feeling of the "square-blade."

Practice

Try putting to a large hatpin stuck into the carpet 3 or 4 feet away and then, as you become proficient, gradually lengthen your distance to 10 or 15 feet. You might place the hatpin directly in front of your ball-return mechanism and give yourself extra credit each time you hit the pin. Always keep score when you practice indoors, just as I suggested you do on the outdoor practice green. See how many out of ten you can score at various distances. And always know at exactly what distance you are practicing. You can actually measure it at home, where you cannot on the course. Such practice will help you to accumulate a store of experience and knowledge which you will be calling upon for answers later on in the golf season.

Work towards a "discriminating" touch, one that can distinguish between a 3-foot putt and a 3½-foot putt. I cannot overemphasize the importance of this, for it is here that you achieve the ability to make the ball "die" at the hole. The practice method I have used for learning this has been to place two pieces of light string parallel to each other and 6 inches apart. Then I putt from about 3 or 4 feet away, first to one and then the other, using about six to eight balls. You will be surprised at how inept you are when you first try this type of practice and how expert you become after you have worked on this for a few weeks. You might even be tempted to get some golfing friend of yours into a little "friendly" match some Saturday night and clean him out.

Another interesting practice technique is to blindfold yourself and putt to a glass tumbler from about 3 feet away. In order to do this, you should get one of those sleeping masks that are complete blindfolds. Put it up on your forehead while you "square" yourself to the ball and your intended line. Then drop the blindfold and putt away. This is wonderful practice for helping you to visualize your square-blade position in the backswing and also to help you to rid yourself of any tendency to look up. For, with nothing to see, and merely the sound of the tumbler to guide you, there is no temptation to look up or move your head as you hit the ball.

All these practice methods and, no doubt, many others that you can invent will help your putting a great deal, even if you devote a very small amount of time to them. Be assured that your practice will pay off in the most satisfying way; the delightful last roll of the ball into the cup for the "sunk" putt.

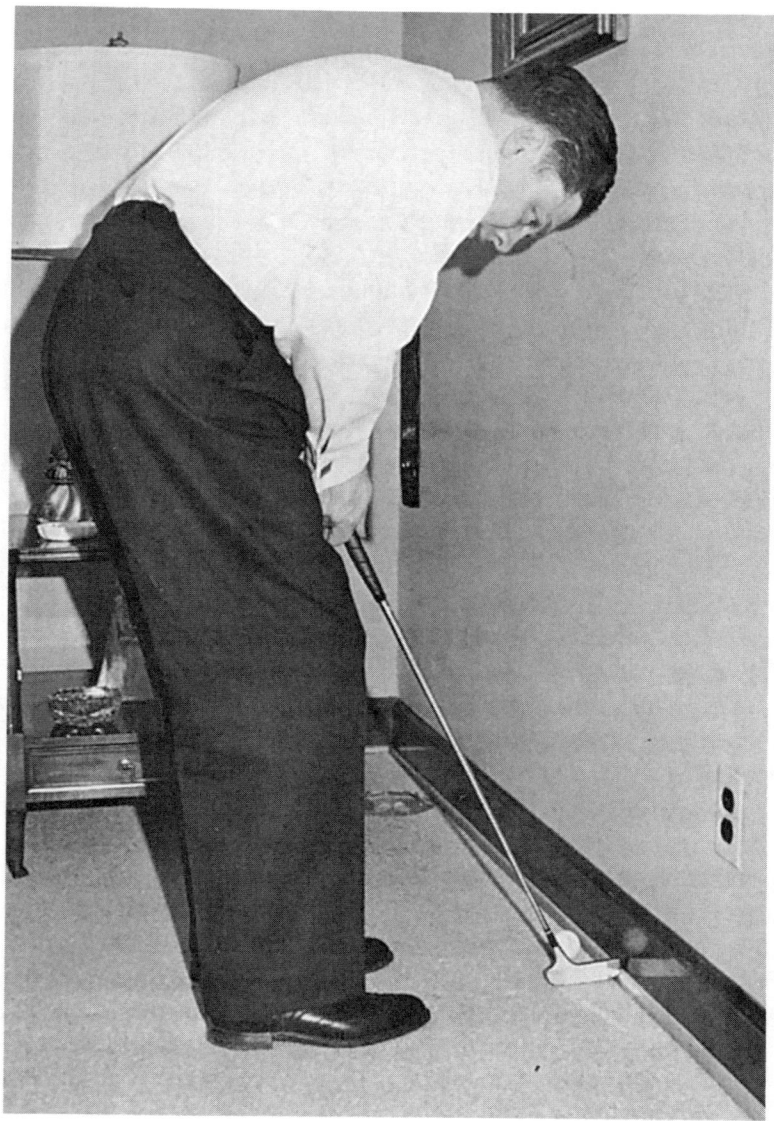

PRACTICING AGAINST A BASEBOARD

This is an excellent and easy way to practice the "square-blade" position, and especially to rid yourself of any tendency to take your blade "out and up." If you put a towel against the wall you can lean your head against the towel and force yourself to keep it still as you putt. It appears that this putting blade is not soled properly. The illusion is due to the carpet's being pinched down near the moulding.

Practice

PRACTICING FOR A DISCRIMINATING TOUCH

By using two pieces of string, parallel to each other and about 6 inches apart, and by putting two balls alternately to one and then the other of these pieces, you will develop a very fine "touch." This same method can be used equally well on the practice green when the weather permits.

Practicing to a Putting Cup at Home

Here is one of the many gadgets for practicing your stroke at home. Note the fine arrangement of right-angled lines. This mechanism is so designed to permit practice from various positions. The ball returns automatically, even when it is holed. Ten minutes a day in the winter will work wonders for your putting game in the summer.

Putting Faults and Their Remedies

How to Take Three Putts

First in addressing the ball for the first putt, stand over it long enough to get completely rigid, if not jumpy in the nerves. . . . Start the backswing with something approaching a swift jerk. Then stab the ball without any attempt at a follow-through, lifting your head and moving your body. This will leave you six or seven feet short of the cup, or five or six feet beyond. . . . Missing the next putt is child's play. Grip the shaft of the putter as tightly as possible. Use another fast, jerky backswing and once more stab the ball as the body moves. This method is sure to leave you another putt of eighteen or twenty inches. You can always increase the number of your putts by increasing the speed of the putting blade and the tightness of your grip. Also by lifting your head and moving your body.

The Duffer's Handbook of Golf

IN MY OPINION, the worst fault in putting is that of rotating the blade of the putter during the backstroke. By doing this, you immediately destroy the true perpendicular alignment of the blade to the line of the putt.

Rotation of the blade, particularly when combined with a lifting of the blade, produces a "cut" or "slice" at the point of impact and prevents the ball from rolling with a desirable overspin. You can remedy this fault by keeping a careful eye on your right hand, and by making sure that both the hand and the palm are facing the hole throughout the stroke. Remember that your right wrist should be arched downward and that only the backward-and-forward hinge of the right wrist should come into play.

Lifting the club head abruptly off the turf at the beginning of the backstroke is another frequent putting error. Often it is combined with the fault of rotation which was just explained, and involves the use of the up-and-down hinge of the right wrist. This fault is apt to cause a pinching effect on the ball and give it an undesirable backspin rather than the desirable overspin. You can correct this fault by concentrating on using the backward-and-forward hinge of the right wrist in "arched" position and also by concentrating on the slight counterclockwise "under" push of the left hand and forearm that I have defined as "hooding." This will help to keep the blade low and level to the turf.

ROTATION AND LIFTING DURING THE BACKSTROKE

Putting Faults and Their Remedies 141

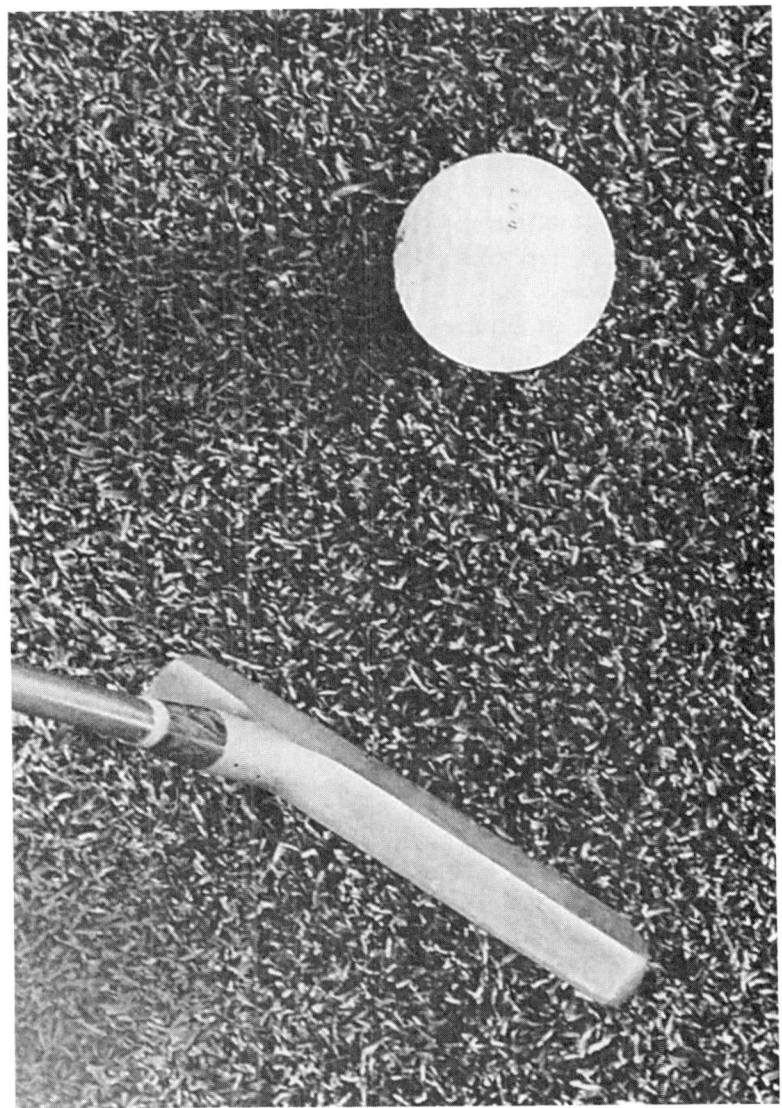

GOLFER'S-EYE VIEW OF ROTATION

142   *The Secret of Holing Putts*

Improper or inconsistent placement of the ball is another common fault that I see in many golfers, especially those with high handicaps. Placing the ball too far back toward the center of the stance will result in a downward stroke at the ball which will give it backspin instead of overspin.

On the other hand, placement of the ball too far forward in the putting stance leads to a tendency for the left wrist to "collapse." The result is a last-minute pull to the left, which, of course, sends the ball in the wrong direction.

In placing the ball, simply be careful to locate it off the inner line of your left shoe. Actually go through the suggested procedure of locating the proper "spot" as shown on pages 48 and 49 until you do it as a matter of instinct.

There are several ways in which faulty use of the hands can cause errors in putting.

BALL PLACED TOO FAR TOWARD CENTER OF STANCE

Putting Faults and Their Remedies

BALL PLACED TOO FAR FORWARD IN THE PUTTING STANCE

The photograph opposite shows the hands too far in front of the ball at the point of impact and the photograph on page 146 shows the hands too far behind the ball. These two faults seriously alter the loft of the blade and result in a faulty roll of the ball. Positioning the hands ahead of the ball causes the "pinching" action that I described earlier, whereas placing the hands behind the ball causes it to be lofted and rolled erratically.

Along with these two faults you will often find another: the failure to have the palms of the two hands directly opposite each other and parallel to the face of the putter. You can remedy this fault by being certain that both thumbs are placed directly on top of the shaft and made to point down the shaft. Make sure that your hands, the direction in which your thumbs are pointing, and the shaft point in the same direction, down the center of the shaft.

Another common fault is related to the amount of pressure exerted by either hand. The amount of pressure with which you grip the club is closely related to the position of the fingers and hands on the shaft. If the grip of the left hand is too loose, the club will be allowed to turn and twist and will not provide proper stability and support for the stroking action of the right hand. You can correct this tendency by stabilizing the left-hand grip, especially in the back part or "heel" of the hand. There should even be the hint of a "squeeze" by the left hand where the shaft runs distinctly into the heel of the hand.

If the right-hand grip is such that the shaft lies mainly across the palm, the essential lightness of touch in the right hand will be lacking. Correct this by making certain that the right-hand grip is entirely in the fingers. This will enhance the light touch which is so vital in estimating correct distance as well as in sensing the position of the blade of the putter.

"Indecision" is another serious putting fault. It usually results from a hurried survey or no survey at all, as, for example, when the player is asked to putt his ball out in order to "clear the cup." Rather than submitting to pressure and putting in a hurry, the player should always mark his ball and give himself sufficient time subsequently to make up his mind how to putt.

It is important to be decisive about both the strength and the "line" of the putt. It is necessary, especially on downhill putts, to decide whether you are going to hit the ball firmly towards the back of the cup and thus ignore the roll or simply "lag the ball" delicately and slowly into the cup. Obviously a "lagged" putt must use more "bor-

Putting Faults and Their Remedies

HANDS TOO FAR IN FRONT OF THE BALL

HANDS TOO FAR BEHIND THE BALL

Putting Faults and Their Remedies 147

row" than a firmly hit one since it will be traveling more slowly and will be more affected by the slope. The remedy for indecisiveness in both these areas is simply to make up your mind what you are going to do and then do it with conviction. If you do become confused when you are about to execute your stroke, step away and reconsider for a moment. When in doubt, hit firmly and allow for less roll than you had originally planned, especially on shorter putts.

Putting Faults Relating to the Stance

Standing too far away from the ball usually results in a tendency to swing with the shoulders and arms rather than with the forearms, wrists, and hands. The latter is far more desirable. An improper stance also places the eyes of the golfer at the wrong angle to the ball and the line of the putt, making it that much more difficult to align the putt.

In order to correct this, the player should assume a position with arms folded. Except on the longer approach putts, there is little need to remove the arms from the body. The eyes should be over the top of the ball so that it is possible to shift them from the ball to the cup and back with ease. By doing this, one can "draw the line" of the putt.

Putting Faults and Their Remedies 149

Freezing

As in all sports, one of the basic faults in putting is the build-up of tension, which causes a "freezing" of the grip and a stiffening of the knees. It is important for you to realize that, especially on long putts, there must be room for movement of the arms. You should therefore not permit yourself to get "locked up" in a cramped position.

The best remedies for tension are deep breathing and a conscious flexibility of the knees. This latter can be accomplished if you get into the habit of "sitting down" to the ball. And always keep in mind those concentric circles, 15, 30, and 45 feet away from the cup. If you do you'll be sure to realize when you are trying to sink a long putt that you need extra freedom of movement.

Confidence

The vital shot—a putt—occurred . . . in the 1929 Open at Winged Foot Club at Mamaroneck, New York. Jones was leading Al Espinosa by four strokes with four holes to go. Then Bob blew, sprinkling 7's around like Rockefeller with a pocket full of dimes. At the 72nd hole he needed a 4 for a tie. Jittery, he left himself a mean 12-foot side-hill putt. With the angel of doom looking over his shoulder, Bob took his Calamity Jane putter, finally stroked the ball . . . and made it! Next day in the 36-hole medal play-off with Espinosa, Jones won by 23 strokes.

"If I'd missed that putt and had lost a tournament already won," commented Jones, "I hate to think of what might have happened to my confidence. And without confidence a golfer is little more than a hacker."

GRANTLAND RICE

"Confidence" in golf is the positive mental attitude which results from the memory of a particular physical action previously accomplished successfully.

Confidence, in my opinion, is closely related to relaxation of the muscles and the mind. It is based upon adequate preparation and constant rehearsal of the particular physical action, under circumstances as closely simulating "pressure" conditions as possible.

Henry Cotton, a great student of golf, has said that you should never putt "in fun," but should always keep yourself "under pressure," if only by betting pennies on your results. For the same reason, I recommend constant rigorous practice at putting, under all possible conditions with respect to the length of the putt, the degree of roll, and the slickness or slowness of the green. In fact, you should practice under as many conditions as your inventive mind can devise.

For when you have successfully holed 10 left-to-right, fast-breaking 3-footers in succession on the practice green and then encounter a similar putt out on the course, the foundation for your confidence has already been laid.

Confidence

Why does a Ben Hogan or a Ken Venturi hit thousands of practice shots a day? Because the golfer who wishes to excel must make the physical action he wishes to accomplish successfully as completely automatic as possible.

The professional of today talks of his "career" shot. By this he is referring to his 2-iron or 4-wood or whatever club he has completely mastered. When he most needs a long shot that carries low to a guarded green he is able to pull out his 2-iron and hit his so-called "career" shot to win. What has he done? He has built confidence in himself, and in his ability to "produce when the chips are down," by daily hitting first twenty out of forty good 2-iron shots, then twenty-five out of forty, then thirty-five out of forty until finally he has reached the point of near perfection. He has laid the foundation for his confidence by instilling in himself the memory of previously successful accomplishments.

So I should like to encourage you to become confident in your putting. You can do it if you will follow the proven method and techniques I have explained to you in this book Practice, practice, practice! Use your intelligence in every putting situation! "Out-think" that green; don't let it beat you. Discover that hidden roll, and that odd twist of grain, and hole that difficult downhill putt! One way you can be sure to do this is by knowing you can do it. You have done it a hundred times before!

Horton Smith's Record

1908	Born Springfield, Missouri, May 22
1926	Turned professional
1928	Oklahoma Open Champion
1929	Pinehurst North and South Open Champion La Gorce Open Champion $5000 Florida Tour Champion Pensacola Open Champion Ft. Myers Open Champion Catalina Open Champion Member, International Ryder Cup Team
1930	Pasadena Open Champion Portland, Oregon, Open Champion Berkeley Open Champion Central Florida Open Champion Savannah Open Champion Third, United States Open
1931	St. Paul Open Champion Member, International Ryder Cup Team
1932	National Capitol Open Champion
1933	International 4-Ball Champion, with Paul Runyan
1934	Masters Open Champion California Open Champion Louisville, Kentucky, Open Champion
1935	Miami Biltmore Open Champion Pasadena Open Champion Member, International Ryder Cup Team
1936	Canadian Victoria Open Champion Masters Open Champion

1937	Runner-up, Western Open
Pinehurst North and South Open Champion
Runner-up (tied), Chicago $10,000 Tour
Co-Winner with Harry Cooper, Toledo Inverness 4-Ball
Co-Winner with Harry Cooper, Oklahoma City 4-Ball
Runner-up (tied), Los Angeles Open
Member, International Ryder Cup Team
1938	Runner-up, Florida Open
Runner-up, Hollywood, Florida Open
1939	Member, International Ryder Cup Team (matches not played)
1940	Colorado Open Champion
Third, United States Open, one stroke back
1941	Massachusetts Open Champion
1942	Member, International Ryder Cup Team (matches not played)
1948	Michigan P.G.A. Champion
1952–54	President, Professional Golfers of America
1954	Michigan Open Champion
1955	Qualified for P.G.A. Championship twenty-first time
1955–57	Honorary President, P.G.A.
1956	Qualified for the United States Open for the twenty-second time
1958	Elected to American P.G.A.'s Golf "Hall of Fame"
Made Honorary Life Member of the P.G.A. of Great Britain
1960	Winner of Ben Hogan Trophy awarded to athlete of the year who makes the greatest contribution to sport in spite of illness

Acknowledgments

Thanks are due to the following authors, publishers, and others for permission to use excerpts from their publications:

Country Life Ltd. and Simon & Schuster, *Bobby Locke on Golf*, copyright © 1954.

Doubleday and Co., Inc., *Golf Is My Game*, Robert Tyre Jones, Jr., copyright © 1960 by Robert Tyre Jones, Jr.

The Macmillan Co., *The Duffer's Handbook of Golf*, Grantland Rice and Clare Briggs, copyright 1926.

G. P. Putnam's Sons, *Down the Fairway*, Robert T. Jones, Jr., and O. B. Keeler, copyright 1927, published by Minton, Balch and Company.

Simon & Schuster, *The Walter Hagen Story*, Walter Hagen, copyright 1956 by Walter Hagen.

United States Golf Association and Cherry Hills Country Club, Denver, Program for 60th Open Championship of the U.S.G.A., 1960.

Bibliography

Advanced Golf, Cary Middlecoff; Prentice-Hall, Inc., Englewood Cliffs, N. J., 1957.

Approaching and Putting, Charles B. Cleveland; T. Y. Crowell Co., New York, 1953.

"The Art of Golf," Sir Walter Simpson, from *Golf,* Horatio G. Hutchinson; Longmans, Green & Co., Inc., London, 1890.

Bobby Locke on Golf, Bobby Locke; Simon & Schuster, Inc., New York, 1954.

Chick Evans' Golf Book, Charles (Chick) Evans, Jr.; The Reilly & Lee Co., Chicago, 1921.

Down the Fairway: The Golf Life and Play of Robert T. Jones, Jr., Robert T. Jones, Jr., and O. B. Keeler; Minton, Balch and Company, New York, 1927.

Driving, Approaching and Putting, Edward Ray; Methuen & Co., Ltd., London, 1922.

The Duffer's Handbook of Golf, Grantland Rice and Clare Briggs; The Macmillan Company, New York, 1926.

From Tee to Cup by the Four Masters, Gene Sarazen, Denny Shute, Ralph Guldahl, Johnny Revolta; Wilson Sporting Goods Co., Chicago, 1951.

The Game of Golf, William Park, Jr.; Longmans, Green & Co., Inc., London, 1896.

The Gate to Golf, J. Douglas Edgar; Edgar and Co., St. Albans, Eng., 1920.

Gene Sarazen and His Pet Ideas, Ernest Heitkamp; Wilson Sporting Goods Co., Chicago, 1932.

The Golfer's Manual, H. B. Farnie; The Dropmore Press, London, 1947.

Golf from a New Angle, Theodore Moore; Herbert Jenkins Ltd., London, n.d.

Golf Is My Game, Robert Tyre Jones, Jr.; Doubleday and Co., New York, 1960.

Golf on the Green, P. A. Vaile; John Wanamaker, New York, 1915.

Golf Putting, L. Art Slack; Indianapolis Printing Co., 1935.

A Guide to Good Golf, James M. Barnes; John Lane, The Bodley Head, Ltd., London, 1929.

How to Improve Your Putting, Bobby Locke; Dunlop Tire and Rubber Corp., Buffalo, N. Y., 1950.

How to Play Your Best Golf All the Time, Tommy Armour; Simon & Schuster, New York, 1953.

How to Putt Better, Innis Brown; M. N. Arnold Shoe Co., South Weymouth, Mass., 1933.

It's the Damned Ball, Ike S. Handy; Anson Jones Press, Houston, 1951.

Low Score Golf, Jim Ferrier; Ziff-Davis Publishing Co., Chicago, 1948.

The Magic of Precision Putting, Lachlan M. Vass, Sr.; Vassco Publishing, New Orleans, 1954.

My Golfing Album, Henry Cotton; Country Life, Ltd., London, 1959.

New Angles on Putting and Chipping, Mark G. Harris; The Reilly & Lee Co., Chicago, 1940.

On and Off the Green, H. A. Hattstrom; The Shoreline Press, Evanston, Ill., n.d.

Practical Golf, Walter J. Travis; Harper & Brothers, New York and London, 1901.

Putting, Jack White; Country Life, Ltd., London, 1921.

Putting and Spared Shots, Abe Mitchell; Methuen & Co., Ltd., London, 1939.

Putting Made Easy: The Mark G. Harris Method, P. A. Vaile; The Reilly & Lee Co., Chicago, 1955.

Scientific Putting, P. A. Vaile; The Beckley-Ralston Co., Chicago, 1927.

Short Cuts to Better Golf, Johnny Revolta and Charles B. Cleveland; T. Y. Crowell Co., New York, 1949.

Success at Golf, Harry Vardon, Alexander Herd, George Duncan, Wilfred Reid, Lawrence Ayton, and Francis Ouimet; Little, Brown & Company, Boston, 1915.

This Game of Golf, Henry Cotton; Country Life, Ltd., London, 1948.

This Is Putting, Louis T. Stanley; H. Allen, London, 1956.

The Tumult and the Shouting: My Life in Sport, Grantland Rice; A. S. Barnes & Co., New York, 1954.

The Walter Hagen Story, Walter Hagen, as told to Margaret Seaton Heck; Simon & Schuster, New York, 1956.

Krista
mattern

Jessica
garbon